This book is a publication of **Legacy X**—

a comprehensive plan for transforming yourself

from the inside out and blasting a permanent

mark into your world. It's a take-no-prisoners

guide to fulfilling your dreams and ambitions by

branding and marketing yourself with rock 'n' roll

energy and warrior tactics.

D1491287

"YOUR LEGACY is your destiny. It's what you were made to do, the fulfillment of your drive to achieve and to succeed. Shed the things you don't need to get the things you do need. Start building the future of your dreams. Reclaim the life that you think has slipped away. Make the change you thought was impossible. You have all the tools you need locked away. Legacy X busts the lock and puts you to work on the great mission of your life, to unleash the person you were meant to be.

"Legacy X is just the operating manual that lets you live so that when you are on your death bed you can look back and say, 'I kicked ass.'"

—Justin Spencer

ONE LIFE,
ONE LEGACY

Justin Spencer

ONE LIFE PUBLISHING
Concord, New Hampshire

Designed and composed at Hobblebush Design, Brookline, New Hampshire (www.hobblebush.com)

Printed in the United States of America

ISBN 978-0-9914637-0-1

Library of Congress Control Number: 2014944397

Published by:

ONE LIFE PUBLISHING
233 South Street
Concord, New Hampshire

www.legacyx.com

Contents

What You Need To Know

IN A TIME when many Americans feel stuck and buried—in debt, overweight, out of shape and out of luck—Legacy X arrives with motivational dynamite to blast them free and clear a path to a dynamic future and leave a unique mark on the world. It's a mark that everyone—young and old—knows is their fundamental right and reason to exist. International performer, speaker and "world's fastest drummer" Justin Spencer is the guide. Spencer shares secrets he's learned while taking his band "Recycled Percussion" from a high school talent show to stardom on the world's largest stage. His methods are a mixture of intimate personal outreach and a scorched earth, take-no-prisoners approach to individual renewal. Spencer invites anyone who feels trapped by habits and blocked by circumstances to start bulldozing their own road to freedom and fulfillment with the power of Legacy X.

Justin Spencer is available as a speaker and motivator for audiences of all ages. Contact him via www.legacyx.com.

The Red Ping Pong Ball

A FRIEND ONCE came to me and said he felt like he was nothing, going nowhere, with no reason to live. I asked him what was wrong and he said it drives him crazy that so many people around him seem to have "charmed lives" while he never gets a break.

I looked him over. He was young, in decent health, had a job, a family, some good friends, even had a car. He had some college and was smart enough to go back if he wanted to. He had all ten fingers and toes.

I told him, "Imagine this. Suppose you're waiting to be born. You aren't anyone yet." He seemed puzzled, but I went on. "To pick the life you are going to live, you've got to dive into a pool filled with thousands of ping pong balls. Each ping pong ball is a different life, some rich, some poor, some sick, some well. There is every kind of life on Earth somewhere in that pool." My friend nodded. I could tell he was imagining some pretty sweet lives, so I told him, "Sure. There are some rich CEOs or athletes and a few movie stars but there are way more crack babies, starving kids in war zones, abused women in tribal Afghanistan, schizophrenics sleeping in the tunnels under Las Vegas, cancer patients in hospice units, ghetto gang bangers, beggars on the streets of Bangladesh, rice farmers in rural Asia, trash-pickers in the slums of Argentina and lots of poor people just struggling to get by without anyone to help them. All you know is you only get one try. You won't have a clue what life you've got until you start to live it—with just one exception. Mixed in with all the others in the pool is just one red ping pong ball. If you get that red ping pong ball, you get some guarantees. You'll live in a wealthy country with freedom to do pretty much whatever you want, you'll have a family, some friends, a healthy body and a good education. You won't be guaranteed to be rich or famous, but there won't be anything stopping you, either. Any other ball is just the luck of the draw. Those are the rules. Now it's your turn and you dive in. You're nervous, but you can't see a thing in there so you just grab one of the balls. When you come to the surface, there in your hand is the red ping pong ball."

The guy just stood there, so I asked him, "Would that make you happy?"

He sort of shrugged and said, "I guess so."

"You guess so?" I said. "Think for just a minute about the millions of people all over the world who don't have a tenth of the shit you have, who would literally give an arm and a leg to live the kind of life you've got. Then think about the billions of people who have lived on the planet over the last 10,000 years, getting eaten by wild animals and dying of the plague or being forced to go to war for cruel dictators or just living in filthy poverty while they watch their babies die from malnutrition. Now, just imagine for a second that all those people are standing around watching you hold that red ping pong ball and listen to you bitch about your life."

As you can see. I'm a sensitive guy, but don't tell me your problems unless you plan to do something about them. Or I'll throw a red ping pong ball at you.

Don't Read This Book!

IF YOU WANT TO SLEEPWALK through another set of guides to success, you are in the wrong place. This isn't a book about reading, it's about doing. Each chapter has more than just information. It has a place to start, something you need to do to get on the path to your Legacy.

AND BEFORE YOU EVEN BEGIN, here's something you need to do. It's an essential first step. If you are serious, ready to go all in, one hundred percent committed to your Legacy then turn the page and do exactly what it says.

OR ELSE JUST PUT THE BOOK BACK on the shelf and come back when you are ready.

Eat
This
Page.*

*OK, on the advice of lawyers and other nervous types, we don't *actually* recommend you eat this page because you might choke and die or break out in hives. (By the way, if you *do* decide to eat it, you're completely responsible for anything that happens to you.) But here's what you *should* do. Tear out this page and do *something* with it—something that makes it a part of your life or makes a permanent mark on your memory. Write a love note on it and send it to someone special, or maybe write a letter to thank your mom for putting up with you. You could tear it into 12 pieces, write your biggest fears on each one and drop them into a river. Maybe burn it and mix the ashes into some paint, then paint a table where you plan to write the Great American Novel. Get creative. Maybe just make an origami animal out of it. Whatever you do, make it memorable. Then, let me know what you did to "eat" this page. Write a note, take a photo or a shoot a video and send it to me at justin@legacyx.com. We'll post the best ideas on the LegacyX.com website.

JUSTIN SPEAKS

Some questions answered by Justin Spencer,
founder of Lecacy X.

Why the X?

MAYBE YOU COULD SAY it's part of a mathematical equation. X equals your worth today times the things that matter to you and it equals what you leave behind—the total impact you have on the world and the lives of others.

Maybe it's a crossroads. X is your decision point. Which path will you take?

Think of it as the spot on the map where the treasure is hidden, because your Legacy is the greatest treasure you will ever find, more valuable than gold, but it's up to you to seek it and dig it out before it's lost and forgotten.

The X is blood red because it means complete commitment, a blood-bond to your Legacy and all that the word indicates. Red is powerful and bold. It's impossible to hide, just like the Legacy you have stashed away inside yourself but that keeps flashing through, keeping you awake, driving you onward.

It's rough and raw, painted in a rush. It could be a mark left by someone in a war zone. Maybe it points out a target or a safe haven. Maybe it's both. It's a mark that belongs on the flag you fly over your home and the one you take into battle because you can't afford to forget it.

It looks urgent, because your situation is urgent. Time is short and it's a life or death matter. It's a call to act, now, while you're alive.

It's all of the above and more, because the final definition of the X is really up to you.

What's Legacy X?

I GET ASKED THIS A LOT. Maybe it's because of the tattoos on my arms, or maybe the T-shirt I'm wearing, or maybe it's because I can't stop talking about it and posting updates about it online.

Sometimes I give them the long version, that Legacy X is a complete program designed to teach you how to realize your personal goal in life. It's also peer-to-peer support that gives you the motivation and the support you need to achieve that goal. It's a website to connect people. It's this book you are reading, plus all sorts of tools designed to keep you focused and on the right track to overhaul your life.

I like the short version better: **It's about helping to create a lifestyle and legacy that you are proud of with a side of badass.**

I came up with this program because it's the story of my own life. I didn't have much going for me and I had plenty going against me when I was a kid. I don't come from money. I don't come from a big town. I wasn't handed a charmed situation. I had a home, like many, where alcohol was a big factor. My parents got divorced. But I didn't focus on the negatives. We used food stamps. Proudly. We needed them. I did what I could to help my family because I loved them. I learned to embrace what I had, not to worry about what I didn't. I'm proud of the life my family lived, problems and all. It built who I am today.

Looking back, I wouldn't change a thing. The life I was born into was my challenge to overcome. It had all the raw materials for my future—the stuff I needed to learn and the kick in the ass I needed to get busy making my own life. I can tell each and *every* one of you that if I can make my passions in life become a daily circumstance and turn *my* dreams into a reality without excuses then *you* can also do the same. Don't think that you have to be lucky or have a gift. You have to truly want it and not stop at any cost until you have it.

This book and the Legacy X movement is part of my dream, my own legacy. I'm not here to tell you what to do, but I may be here to help you figure it out on your own terms.

I haven't gotten where I am today by compromising with anyone who thought they knew more about my life than I do. I've learned something from everyone in my life but I've never let anyone tell me how to live it, so I'm not going to compromise here, either. The language in this book may be a little raw, but it's the way I talk. If I seem overexcited about the possibilities, it's because I think they are that exciting. If it seems like I'm asking a lot of people, well I am, but no more than I expect of myself.

I don't like self-help books. I don't read them. When

I was first thinking about this book I went to a bookstore and took all the motivational, self-help books I could off the shelves and spread them out on a table. On the covers I saw a lot of promises—mostly about health and weight and money. Lots of the titles used numbers like the "Seven Laws of Success" or the "80/20 Principle." People like numbers. They are easy to understand.

On the author's pages I saw a lot of well-dressed people with expensive haircuts and big smiles. I could imagine these people talking to huge audiences of other people who looked just like them, trying to be just like them, richer, thinner, more famous. What I didn't see anywhere in those books was normal people, regular folks in suburbs and trailer parks and high rises, struggling with everyday problems and trying to get by.

This is a book for those regular people. No one is here to tell you what your dreams should be. No one can assign you your Legacy. That's your job. No one can give you what you need to achieve your Legacy, because all you've got to have is what's inside you already. You have the stuff it takes to be the person you are meant to be, and you won't get there by comparing yourself to someone else. But everyone can use a little help. That's why we're here. To help each other out along the way.

Legacy X is a movement of regular people remembering who they are, what dreams they have bottled up inside them and determined to let those dreams out where they can live and breathe. A big part of the movement is getting together with others, to hold each other accountable, to tell each other what they've learned along the way, to make the going easier for the next guy.

A while ago I was asked to write an editorial for my local paper, the *Las Vegas Sun*. It appeared in a column that's usually written by Robin Leach (the guy with the British accent who made "Lifestyles of the Rich and Famous"). Leach was taking some time off and the paper was asking Las Vegas personalities and performers to fill in. I wrote this without even mentioning Legacy X, but if you want the real long answer to the question "What is Legacy X," this is probably as clear as it gets, because it's not really about explaining things. It's about doing things. Read it over. Try the exercise at the end. Then let me know what happened when you met the real you.

●

Many of us wake up every day with a clouded sense of direction. We start our days gearing up for lives we aren't sure we want to be living. We hustle to ensure that we aren't late for jobs we don't enjoy, to see people who pretend to care about us and to work another day fulfilling someone else's dream.

This is a nails on a chalkboard lifestyle. I am here to reinforce the fact that this lifestyle doesn't need to exist.

While we think this is our life, it's not. Nobody is making us get up every day and do this. We are choosing to out of fear, insecurity and lack of confidence in our own abilities to garner more out of ourselves.

I personally had every reason to fail, just like many of you may have. I grew up poor with substance abuse prevalent in my house. I grew up in a small town with little hope of making the kind of life I desired for myself.

We can't keep waking up every day to live a life that isn't ours. We need to take control of what we can control, and that's ourselves.

Take my job with Recycled Percussion as an example. My actual job is performing nightly as a headliner at The Quad, but there is so much more I have to do to prepare for and promote this show.

I am fortunate enough to be able to incorporate some of my passions, like drumming and an active lifestyle, into the show. I also have to put in the time at the gym and concentrate on a healthy overall lifestyle so I can best perform for our fans who come from all over the world to see our performances.

Through hard work, dedication and the determination to never give up, I have been able to make my dream a reality and escape the life my previous surroundings could have led me to; this took great focus. Because it has worked for me, I encourage you to pursue your goals and focus on how you are going to get to where you want to be.

Do me a favor: Today, shut your phone off for 30 minutes

and find a place to be alone. Sit in your car or walk to a park. Flush your mind of the life you are currently living. Say to yourself, "If you could scorch Earth, how would you start over? Where would you go?"

Find that thought process that gives you butterflies in your stomach. Find that something that truly makes you smile. That, my friends, is the true you and the answer for which you are looking.

Don't turn around and say, "Well I can't do it; it's impossible." This is the thought process that's gotten you into this mess in the first place. We all possess the inner power to change the aspects of our lives we are dissatisfied with; we just need to realize it.

So today (not tomorrow!), try the aforementioned exercise, and I think you will be shocked to meet the real you. I promise that it's in there somewhere. Find yourself, be yourself, for yourself.

●

So that's your first exercise. You need to do it. Give yourself 30 minutes to rethink everything in your life. And know this is true: Whatever change you would make, whatever direction you wish you could have taken. You can.

And that's the beauty of it. You are free to change. It's never too late.

You can be proud of who you are and what you do, starting now.

You can defeat or outsmart any obstacle that stands in your way. Others will see where you are going and will be inspired to set their own goals, to find their own stories, to overhaul their own lives, because this kind of action is contagious. Once you start you'll find new obstacles but also new tools and new friends to overcome them.

And as you overcome, you will live the kind of life that you are happy to wake up to—every single day.

Because that's your true Legacy.

And, that's it, your introduction to Legacy X. This book is full of useful tools, serious advice and powerful motivation. Trust me, it doesn't mean shit if you are still just sitting on the pot. But, if you're ready to rock, start reading. If you want more, go to legacyx.com, drop me a line and let's do this thing.

—Justin Spencer, Las Vegas, Nevada

Your Legacy

YOU ARE DYING.

That's the good news.

If you are dying it means one thing: You aren't dead yet.

So you've got some time. Could be minutes. Could be days. Could be decades.

But make no mistake, just because you are alive doesn't mean you are living.

People who hear a doctor say "You've got cancer" usually think that those three words are the worst thing a person could hear. But after the news sinks in they realize that it was the best thing that ever happened to them. Sure there's sadness, fear, maybe some pain, but there's also power. There's nothing like facing death to make you really want to live.

Nobody wants to die, but do you really want to live? Do you want to experience life the way it's supposed to be— an incredible adventure—one mind-boggling miracle after another—a chance to make a difference and to leave a mark on the world? Or do you want to just keep hitting the snooze button over and over until it's all gone. If you want to wake up and choose life, here's more good news.

You can.

In fact, it's what you were designed to do. And there's only one thing that can keep you from living that kind of life.

You.

It's completely up to you. You want it, you can have it. You don't want it and you can hang around and take up space for whatever time you've got.

So how much time have you got?

Not much.

Life, even a long life, goes by in a blink. It may not seem like it now, but it will when it's about to end. You'll know then that every second was precious. You may not regret the times you kicked back and relaxed, watched the clouds roll by or slept in on a Saturday morning. You will regret the months and years you spent sleepwalking through your life in a world full of opportunities that you hardly ever took the time to notice.

This is the truth: no matter how young or healthy you are, whatever time you have left is short. You need to get started.

"This is your life, and it's ending one minute at a time." That's a quote from *Fight Club*, my favorite movie. It reminds me that life can be like watching a timer tick down to zero. Then what? An explosion? The cake is done? Doesn't matter, because you're gone. It's a thought that should make you ask yourself, "Why am I sitting here staring at the timer?"

Maybe you think you've got nothing better to do than watch time pass. You're wrong. You've got a mission. It's something that you were designed to do. Only you can do it but it's way bigger than you.

Want to know what it is? You should.

The entire history of the world, from the Big Bang to the dinosaurs to the Dark Ages to the Industrial Revolution to the Computer Age—all that happened just to get to this place and time, to set things up for this moment for you to hear this message. All that happened just to give you a chance to show what you're made of, to see if you can really stake your claim, rise and shine, save the day.

It's like the last scene of a great movie. Everything has built to this moment and everything depends on you. Imagine you're an international spy who has only seconds to cut the wire to a nuclear bomb, or the scientist working on the antidote to a global plague before it contaminates the world. You are at a turning point in history. Right this moment you are on the cutting edge of time and space, and you have a decision to make.

Do you act, or do you choke?

Some Perspective

So you're thinking, "Bullshit. There are millions of people out there with more important jobs than me. What can I do that would make much difference in the world?"

I say that's bullshit. That's a lazy excuse. That's the part of you that wants to stay asleep and hit the snooze button on your life for another year or two.

We're talking about *your* world.

It's *your* life that's ticking away, ending one second at a time. If you don't take action in time the nuclear bomb goes off, the plague infects the world, the bad guys win. Game over.

The movie *Schindler's List* is about the Holocaust where millions were killed and this one guy repeats an old Jewish saying which means, "Save one life and you save the whole world." While millions are dying, what different can one life make? Oskar Schindler saved hundreds of Jewish people's lives in the middle of Nazi Germany. Who knows what some of those people went on to do. They lived their lives, had children, raised families, opened businesses. We can't judge how important a person's life is. We can only judge if we are living up to our own dreams, fulfilling our own goals. So maybe the only life you save is your own, but that's enough. Who knows what effect your life can have if you are truly living, doing the things that only you can do.

So everyone is in the same situation, but as far as you are concerned there's nothing more important in the whole world, or in the history of the world, than that you get this thing right and seal the deal, and that you do it now. You are either in the game or not.

If you are in, you add something unique to the world and to everything and everyone in it.

If you are not, then you are just dead weight. You are a burnt out bulb on the marquee of life. You can stay up there a long time before someone bothers to replace you, but you are basically dead already.

Legacy What?

So, what is this big world-changing mission?

Just like any hero in any movie you've ever seen, you've been called to the rescue. You may be waiting for a message from God, or from Obi Wan Kenobi or the President, but you've heard this message since you were a kid. It's written in your DNA.

It's why you're here.

That's why it's *your* mission. It's something that only *you* can do. It's your Legacy. The first thing you've got to do is wake up and the next part of your mission is to get ready. You've got to use what you've got, get focused, get stronger, get organized. You need to stop making excuses for yourself or being satisfied with just getting by. You need to look for others who are on their own missions, to learn from them and help them along the way. You need to take your stand and save the world, just in the nick of time.

Your Legacy is what you were made to do and this book is a set of tools to help you on the way, to keep you motivated and aware. No one can tell you exactly what your Legacy is. Part of your job is to figure that out. But here are some clues.

Are you good at something? That's part of your Legacy. Are you, or were you ever, passionate about something? That passion is what you'll need to fuel your Legacy. Was there a dream you had as a kid? Something you knew was out there, waiting for you? That was your first glimpse of your Legacy. Is there something you've always wanted to achieve, but just never could find the time? That's you putting off your Legacy.

Most importantly, is there something you'd live for and die for?

That's your Legacy.

If you are still reading, it's because you recognize those clues. It may not be clear to you yet, but you have an idea of what you need to be doing with your life. You also feel deep in your soul that if you aren't working on your passions or trying to make them the center of your life, then right now you are just watching the clock tick down.

If you're still reading then there's hope. You are on the move. You are on the mission.

You just need to get ready to go balls to the wall for your Legacy.

Promises, Promises

Lots of books like this make big promises. "Become a Genius While You Sleep!" "Earn a Million Dollars in One Year!" "Lose Weight While Watching Television!"

Chances are you're smart enough not to believe every promise you see on the cover of a book, but I'm going to promise you something: If you go all in for your Legacy you'll get it. If you quit fucking around and make your passion the center of your life, then your life will change for the better. And if you feed that passion, even if it's just a spark, it will burst into flame and light up the world, big time. It's like magic.

People think of magic as something that's easy. You just wave a wand and say the magic word and a rabbit pops out of the hat. Real magic takes work, but the results are not tricks, they are transformations. You have to take shit and make it into gold.

Don't think it's possible?

What do you call it when someone has a dream, a plan, that they never do anything to make happen.

You call it bullshit.

I don't really like the word "dream." People say it when what they mean is a "plan." It's something they want to happen. Dreams are about sleeping. Plans are about waking up and smelling the coffee. When you have somewhere you want to go, you come up with a plan and, just like magic, you are on the path to it. You may have a terrible plan, but you just turned shit into gold. You can work a plan. You can improve it. You can't do shit with a dream.

A plan is a path and being on the path is practically the same as getting there. Think about it. A path is a real connection to your goal. Follow it far enough and you're there. Right? Well, wrong. Because the truth is you never really *arrive*. When you get to where you want to go, the first thing you learn is that it's just a new place to start. Reality is that you are always moving until you die. That's all the more reason to move. People aren't things. You are not what you *are*. What you are is a big bag of skin filled with water and chemicals. People *are* what they *do*. Do the right stuff and you are on the right path and if you are on the right path, along the way you become a trendsetter and a leader. Choose a path and stick with it and people start to follow you. You become a leader. Along the way you may even become a legend, but you damn sure achieve your Legacy.

Your Legacy becomes a personal brand that is memorable and powerful and that will live on even after you are gone.

This process takes time and effort, but it's guaranteed to work because it's based on the way the world actually operates. Your dreams aren't illusions that distract you from reality. Your "dreams" (those things that give you butterflies, that pull at your heart, that keep you up at night) are reminders that you have to start making plans. They are pointers to the reality that's meant to be, just waiting for you to step up and create it.

People are basically Legacy machines. It's what human beings do. It's what separates us from everything that makes up the rest of the universe. All the stuff around you, big and little, stars, planets, animals, geology, chemistry, math and any other thing you can name plays a role, but they are all just details, plot devices, props in a great story. Other people are part of your story, too, but they have stories of their own. What separates us from the great story of the universe is that we are also storytellers. The world is bigger than us. In fact, it's so much bigger that it might not seem like you matter. But this is where size really doesn't matter. You may just be a fleck of dust, but unlike everything else we know, you get to decide what you are and what you'll become. Our hopes and our plans are the most powerful forces in the universe because we have the ability to make them come true.

This isn't about your ego. You aren't any better than anyone else. And no one is perfect. We all have limitations, handicaps. But do you want to be defined by your limitations or defined by your ability to overcome them? The choice is yours. Why not define yourself by your dreams, passions and highest aspirations and then set out to achieve them?

When you go for your Legacy, your experiences will grow richer, your relationships will grow deeper, your work will become more meaningful and you will feel fulfilled and purposeful in the things you want to do and the things you have to do.

Like I said, this magic isn't easy. In fact it will be the hardest thing you've ever done, but nothing else will ever satisfy you like going for your Legacy, because it will be the work you were born to do.

And it's never too early or late to begin.

Maybe you're just a kid and your parents don't think you can cross the street by yourself, but you can start the biggest adventure of your life in your own backyard (or like me, in your own basement). Maybe you're old. You're nearing retirement. You're afraid to risk losing the life you've built. But if it's not what you want to be doing, you can use the time you have left to start a whole new life. It's still waiting for you to start building it. You may feel like you aren't ready yet or that you've taken too long to start or maybe you're waiting for some big secret to be revealed, but there really is no secret. You just need to seek and you will find.

This book is designed to start you on your search and then to help you on your way. You may not need much help or you may need a lot, so this book is part of a program designed to give you just what you need to get started, tools to help you grow and directions to find more resources.

If you've come this far, then there's no reason to turn back. Take the Legacy X challenge and you can expect to look back at this moment as a turning point in your life—the beginning of a revolution that will change everything.

It's a revolution that begins the minute you know that you are dying.

MEET THE

MEGANODES

WTF is a Meganode?

HAVING LEVERAGE MEANS having some powerful influence. If you know the right place to push you can knock down a giant. A philosopher named Archimedes once said "Give me a lever long enough and I can move the world." A Meganode isn't about moving the world, exactly. It's about something even tougher. It's about getting yourself off your ass to make a powerful move in the right direction. Each Meganode is a place you can push yourself and get those kinds of results.

A "node" is a place where two or more things connect. A Meganode is a place where *all* the connections of your life come together. It's a place of power that allows you to take control, to rearrange your life and rise to the top of your game. I've studied life-changing action my whole life. I came from a broken home in a small New Hampshire town and I've headed up a revolution in music that has put me and my band, Recycled Percussion, in front of some of the world's largest audiences and earned us a starring role in Las Vegas, the live entertainment capital of the world!

Think of it like this: Goffstown, New Hampshire, where I grew up, is a node. Las Vegas, New York City, Paris or Dubai, those are Meganodes. There are nodes and Meganodes all over the place, even inside you. But you don't have to travel to get to your own Meganodes, you just have to learn to recognize them.

Each of the following chapters is about an incredible power point, but it's also about a starting point. But we're not talking about starting on a trip to the store or going on a vacation. You are taking the first steps on the road to your destiny. The most powerful step is the first one because without it you just stay in the same place. The Meganodes can get you up and going and can supercharge every step you take. There's nothing wrong with Goffstown, New Hampshire. It's my home town. I love it. It will always be part of me. But you can't stay at home if you want to go places with your life.

Each Meganode in this book is an essential tool to life on every level. Just like the capitals of the world, they are all connected. Work with any one of these Meganodes long enough and it will eventually lead you to the others. But why wait for that? Here they are all in one place—the tools you need to move your world with your own bare hands.

"Your time is limited, so don't waste it living someone else's life. Don't be trapped by dogma—which is living with the results of other people's thinking. Don't let the noise of others' opinions drown out your own inner voice. And most important, have the courage to follow your heart and intuition. They somehow already know what you truly want to become. Everything else is secondary."

—Steve Jobs

Meganode 1 — The Truth

ALL I NEEDED WAS ONE OF THOSE big cardboard tubes of Lincoln Logs, a bucket of Legos, some G.I. Joes, my record player and a half a dozen flashlights. While my friends were out on their bikes or playing in the dirt, I was dimming the basement lights and launching my career as a musician and music producer. I was 5 years old.

It wasn't a straight line from that darkened basement to a Vegas stage. After creating those concerts with my G.I. Joes strutting on a Lincoln Log stage and Pink Floyd blasting on my cheap speakers, I moved up in the entertainment world. I'd put on shows for my parents or when they'd have friends over. They say I was a real ham, but I felt like a star. My dad encouraged me. Sometimes he would even accompany me on his drums while I'd stand like Elvis Presley and strum a giant guitar.

I was used to playing on secondhand equipment, borrowed stuff, so it was natural to start playing percussion on just about anything that was lying around. When I started my band, Recycled Percussion, in 1995, that's what we did, working plastic buckets and old car parts into the act. I called it "junk rock," and the band really found a groove and started building an audience. For a while things seemed good and got pretty exciting, but by 1999 the band had broken up—or maybe we just shut down. We'd only really been performing around New Hampshire, playing local high school concerts, sometimes just for lunch money, and appearing at Odyssey of the Mind events. We'd made a few hundred dollars here and there, but it was time to go to college. I had bills to pay so I got a job working in the meat room at Sam's Club.

What I remember most about my time in school was sitting in class, getting itchy, unable to focus. Nothing in class sparked an interest in me. I wondered if I was in the right major. I had no passion no matter what was the subject. I wondered if I was going to college for me or if it was just something to make my parents happy. I knew what I wanted was to be on stage. I wanted to be in a band. All I thought about was playing music. I knew I loved to learn but I hated school which just left me more confused.

Then came a moment I remember like it was yesterday.

I was snoozing through a business law class (a subject that would probably come in handy for me now) and I had to go to the bathroom. Afterwards, instead of going back to my desk I went out to my car. My ride was a 1988 red Ford Escort. It was covered with bumper stickers for rock bands I loved. I can't remember exactly what was going through my head, but I had one of those old Tandy cell phones the size of a brick so I pulled it out and called one of the members of Recycled Percussion. Calls cost 29 cents. Texting hadn't been invented.

I got my friend on the phone, leaned against a light pole, and said, "Hey man, I don't know what's going on with you, but I know this isn't who I am. We've got to get the band back together." Just saying those words out loud turned on the lights. Immediately, got this butterfly feeling in my guts. There was no turning back. I felt liberated.

I didn't know why I was unhappy until I knew what made me happy.

The following day I withdrew from school—then I told my dad. While he always encouraged music, he also always encouraged a backup education. But I knew to be successful in music I had to give it 100 percent. I knew if I had a fallback, I'd use it, so I was going in no-holds barred.

This all took place in a matter of hours. I felt no fear. I probably should have. It was still two years before we got a break and started going places, but I knew in that moment, regardless of whether or not the band became a success, I had succeeded already. Even if I came up short I had won, because at last I was being true to myself.

I'm not saying there are any guarantees. Trying to be a professional musician is probably one of the most risky choices you can make. And I lived in New Hampshire—not a hotbed of music opportunities—and I had no money and no connections. But I had connected to something more important than money. I'd connected to the truth.

I like to tell people not everyone can be a rock star but you can be a rock star at whatever you do. If you're going to be a landscaper then do it like a rock star. What makes rock so cool is that it's about people with passion who believe in what they are doing and have thrown themselves into it completely. If you are doing something you really want to do, you'll have passion. There are a lot of jobs out there, so you might as well do one you want to do, because that's where you will find your own butterflies.

Everyone has a path to follow, but it's easy to get derailed. I knew I was a musician when I was 5 and I know it now. That's the true me.

Today I build my Lincoln Log sets on the Las Vegas Strip.

Wake Up and Smell the Honesty

If you died today, would you be happy with what you left behind? Would there be something on the table, something important to you that you haven't done yet?

I'm not saying you haven't done some good stuff in your life. Who cares? Not relevant. That's what you're supposed to be doing. The question is how can you leave the mark you were made to create? That's your assignment. You don't have time to waste patting yourself on the back.

You need to have a purpose in life, commit to it and go for it with all you've got. Anything less than that and you are basically just part of the furniture. If you can't aspire to something great, then why even live? Ask yourself that question. No one is going to ask it for you.

Truth is, the only person who really cares about the true you is you. I'm not talking about people who love you. You may have lots of people who love you, but only you know or care about your own Legacy because that's what it is. It's yours and yours alone. Everyone else you know is in exactly the same boat. We can support each other along the way, but in the end it's not up to someone else to define who you are or what you become.

Truth is square one. You have to start somewhere and the first place to begin changing things is to admit how they really are. Unfortunately the simple truth is hard to come by and way too rarely heard, even from your friends. And, admit it, you aren't that straight with yourself, either.

Are you really honest with yourself? What's the bullshit you sell yourself every day? What are your excuses? You probably have enough of them to fill a library and you have them alphabetized for easy access so you know where to find them. I'm here to tell you to dump that entire library in a trash heap and set it on fire.

If you want to find out how honest you are to yourself, here's an easy test. Make three short lists:

1. Your biggest hopes and plans and the things you really most want to do;

2. The things that stop you from doing what you
   want;
3. The things you are doing to break through those
   barriers.

The first list should be easy. Put it all down— travel to another country, learn to play cello, run your own company, have a bunch of kids—whatever. The second one might take more thought, but put it all down so you have a real inventory of every limitation or problem that stands in your way. The last list is the important one. If that last list doesn't have something on it that you've done today or yesterday, or at least this week, then face it. You're lying to yourself. Maybe you are lying about your dreams. Maybe you don't really care that much about them and you're fooling yourself when you say you want to make things happen, to do better and be a stronger person. Or maybe you are lying to yourself about what's stopping you. Maybe you are blaming other people or situations for holding you back and really just giving up.

Who Are You, Anyway?

It's possible that you are lying every time you introduce yourself. You say, "Hi, I'm——." But you're really just repeating a name out of habit. What does that name stand for? What's the stuff you are made of? Where are you going and where do you want to go? Maybe you once knew the

Open Your Eyes

magine a world where you wake up and the first thing that pops into your mind is bliss. Not for a day, not because its a holiday, your birthday or a special day but because it's just any other day. Imagine that those days repeat themselves, over and over, you wake up a little stronger than the morning before, your purpose is building, the light is getting brighter and your world is coming into focus. Things are clicking, the answers to questions you desire are in front of you and more clear than ever. Well don't imagine that anymore, live that! Feel that! Believe in that! Because its 100 percent within your reach. Not every day will you wake up in a bedroom full of flowers, but certainly every day you wake up you have a *choice* of finding bliss. Even in a dark day, even if your day starts by fighting a traffic ticket or going to the dentist. You can still look at life as the "big picture." You can look past the speed bumps of hell in front of you and see the autobahn of life, the open road of a new-found freedom that you control. It's *never* too late and *never* impossible to make what I just suggested become a reality. So start your Friday morning in a state of bliss no matter what the day brings. You change the future by seeing the now with new eyes.

answers back when you were a kid, but who the fuck are you now?

From all the times I've asked that question of people I can conclude one thing: chances are you are not who you want to be.

If you aren't working on that—becoming the person you want to be, then all your hopes and plans are really just bullshit.

And the only person you are fooling is you.

The truth is that the main thing keeping you from your goals and aspiration is just you, your own choices, attitudes and behavior. And that's the one problem that is completely in your hands to solve.

Do you want a different career, working on something that you love doing? Do you want to lose weight, be more fit, think clearer, get more done in a day? There are things you can do right now—every single day—to make that all happen. Unless you are in jail or the hospital, you have absolute control over your own time, your own body, the choices you make in what you eat, how often you exercise, what you learn and where you put your attention. And even if you are in jail, even if you live in a slave labor camp in North Korea, you can still control what you think and how you behave.

Only you are in control of you. Stop fooling yourself. Snap out of it.

The Truth about People

Everyone has responsibilities. So you can't just blow off work early and go to the gym whenever you like, but you sure can get some exercise before or after work every day. You've got a family? You've got family obligations? Do them, then go to the gym, and pick up some healthy food on the way home so you don't just eat a box of ice cream. You like ice cream. Great. Set a goal at the gym, achieve it, then enjoy an ice cream cone. You've earned it.

It's not rocket science. It's just common sense. But we get so good at lying to ourselves that after a while we start to believe the biggest lie. It's the lie that says that we can't control what we do with our bodies or what we put into them or how we manage our time. It's a lie we tell ourselves.

The bigger the lie, the stronger the truth you need to expose it. The absolute strongest truth is this: You are in control of your own life. If you're buried, start digging out. If you are fucking up, then stop it. Now. Start over. Get it right. Do it now.

Where do you start? Don't let the mess you are in become the excuse for not getting started. Just do the one thing that's right in front of you. Can't see the thing that's right in front of you? Then go get your eyes examined.

Here's a secret that everyone knows. It's only a secret because it's so easy to forget.

Once you start doing something it gets easier.

This is true whether you start playing the drums or pumping iron. It's also true about lying on the couch. It gets easier once you start. Don't underestimate this power. Use it. You get to decide what you want to make easier. If you have a major life goal it's going to take time, sure, but you can be on the road today, right now, by just taking a step. Then, the next time someone asks who you are and where you are going, you'll have an answer.

It only takes one step to be on the road somewhere.

But be warned. The same principle that gets you on the road to getting better applies to every bad habit. If you make a decision that makes an easy thing easier—like say taking drugs or watching TV, that will happen too. Do it long enough and it will make you weaker. But if you start doing something that's hard to do—something you don't really want to do, but that you know will take you where you want to go, something like working out, or eating right or getting smarter—if you make something like that easier then you get strong. Then you start to change your world.

See, it's easy. Take one step in the right direction, and then another, and another.

That's how you learned to walk when you were a baby, and that's how you learn to start walking now. It's just that now you are taking bigger steps and going to places that really matter.

Can't think of where to start? It's too complicated? Try this. Write this down on a piece of paper and hang it over your TV and on your refrigerator and anywhere else you spend too much time: "Stop Lying to Yourself! You are in Control of You!"

Remember: Life is short and then you die. You don't know when, but you know you aren't going to be around forever. And then it's game over. You've had your chance.

So why do you live like you have all the time in the world?

No matter how short it is, the life that you've got to live is something incredibly valuable. Astronomers think there must be life on other planets. Maybe in the billions of galaxies out there there's life everywhere, but as far as we know right now, this is it. As far as you are concerned, your life is the absolute rarest most precious thing in the entire universe and it's ticking away. So get off your ass and stop wasting it. If you are just killing time, waiting around to die, the truth is you are dead already.

The Truth about the Universe

The universe is a big place full of lots of stuff. It's mostly full of energy—stars, quasars, black holes, radiation. And there's lots of raw materials. Name the rarest element you can think of and somewhere in the universe there's a whole planet made out of it.

So there's all that energy and all that stuff out there, but there's only one thing we know that can actually take that power and that stuff and make it into something. I'm not talking about planets and stars. I mean something like a good meal, or a drum solo, or a skyscraper. The only "thing" in the universe that can do that is a person like you. Your body and mind working together become one of the most amazing things in the entire known universe. It doesn't matter who you are. This is true if you are Matt Fucking Damon or Joe Schmo.

You have incredible power at your fingertips. The power to change things—for better or for worse.

It sucks that some people use this power to make the world a shittier place, to kill or destroy or treat other people like they are inferior. But to have that kind of energy and all the potential around you and just let your life drift by, that's a crime, too. In fact it makes sense for bad people to do bad shit. At least it shows some initiative. But for a decent person to waste the chance to be better, to not even try to make the most of what they've been given, that may be a bigger crime.

You owe it to the universe, you owe it to yourself to take responsibility for the incredibly rare opportunity— the gift—of being alive.

Remember the story of the red ping pong ball?

You live in America? You're in pretty good health? You've got a high school education? Billions of people would give their right arm up to the shoulder for what you've got. And no matter how much more or less you've got than anyone else, it's your job to do the best you can with it. And it helps to realize that there's so much more out there if you start looking for it. Once you start taking responsibility for your gifts, the world becomes a much bigger and more exciting place. New opportunities open up when you look for them just as surely as they go away if you sleep through them.

You snooze, you lose. Whoever said that is a fucking genius.

If you want to be alive, not just breathing, then you need to understand the potential you possess and start to work it. Once you start anything it gets easier and you get better at it. And if you start doing one thing every day to make yourself better, it adds up. Imagine that you are walking with a crowd of people all day, but every ten minutes or so you jog for about 20 steps. Nothing strenuous. You just put a little extra oomph into every ten minutes. By the end of the day, you'll have left the crowd so far behind you won't see them.

You can start any time. The longer you wait, the harder it gets to start but the power to choose which way to go is all yours. That's the truth.

And the truth really will set you free.

It will set other people free as well. You can't make decisions for people or tell them what to do, but you can start giving them accurate information to work with. Give people around you some truth. It's good medicine. You don't have to be an asshole about it. I should also point out it's a big mistake to start being honest with other people before you get honest with yourself. That's what's known as a hypocrite. But even when it's harsh, sometimes the best thing you can do for someone is tell them something they don't want to hear. Maybe they'll return the favor. Maybe you'll learn something.

When Steve Jobs was the CEO of Apple he made it his business to tell people exactly what he thought. It sometimes turned people against him, and for awhile it even got him fired at Apple, the company he'd created. Some people called him a bully. But people always knew what he really thought. And he wasn't being a jerk just to put people down. He knew where he wanted to go, he knew his time to get there was limited, and he didn't want to waste time with bad ideas.

Jobs knew his business was all about coming up with what he liked to call "insanely great ideas"—ideas that would change the world. He thought that goal was important enough that it if he offended some people along the way, it was worth it. In the long run he pissed off a lot of colleagues but he also attracted a certain kind of people around him. These were people who could take a hit. They could listen to his honesty and they eventually learned to be honest with him as well. When he rebuilt Apple Computers with that group of people around him they were tapped into incredible power. Working with truth, the process to making good ideas into even better realities got faster and more creative. The world was changed.

If you want to change the world, even if you just want to get off your butt and justify your sorry existence, you've got to dig for the truth. Are you content heading down a road of mediocrity, carrying yourself along like a bag of rotten meat on its way out to the dumpster or do you want to stand up and be alive, chart your own course and tell the world why you are here?

This is a gut check moment, a call to action. Your chance to commit to opening your mind over the rest of this book. You wouldn't have read this far if you didn't know that you are in a world of shit and in need of help. Step one is you've got to decide. Are you in? Are you one hundred percent on board with becoming who you know you can be?

I sincerely hope so, because this might be your last chance.

And that's the truth.

Actions

1. "Who are you?" Ask yourself that question and write down your answer. Don't write down who you used to be or who you see yourself being in ten years. Who are you right now?
2. Find out how honest you are being with yourself. Make three lists: 1. The things you really most want to do 2. The things that are keeping you from doing what you want, and 3. The things you are doing to break through those barriers.
3. Immediately do one thing to break through one of your barriers.

Strategies

(Got a plan? A crazy idea? A way to fix the world?
Write that shit down and do it!)

_____
_____
_____
_____
_____
_____
_____
_____
_____
_____
_____
_____
_____
_____
_____
_____
_____
_____
_____
_____
_____
_____
_____

"You may ask yourself;
'How did I get here?'"

—Talking Heads, "Once in a Lifetime"

Meganode 2 — The Paths

WHEN I WAS IN 6TH GRADE, things cost less than today. The average price of a car was less than $10,000 and movie tickets cost about three bucks. Lunches at my school were 75 cents. I paid a lot of attention to money, because I didn't have much back then and I noticed something. My friends almost always paid for their lunches with a dollar. Almost no one ever just carried three quarters. So the cafeteria cash register handed out a quarter in change to just about every kid.

I was always looking for angles, ways to make a little extra money, but this seemed like more than just a petty cash deal. It seemed like a chance to do something really big. One day I got an idea. There were lots of kids who I knew had to get their lunches subsidized by the school. I knew a lot of them didn't have much food at home either. With a whole line of kids, every day getting handed a quarter back from their lunch money, why not give them something to do with that quarter to help out their friends, even before they had a chance to put it in their pockets? My idea was to put a bucket at the end of the line to collect money for kids whose families couldn't afford presents at Christmas. I wasn't shy. I pitched the idea to the principal and he loved it. We wound up raising about a thousand dollars for a local charity. I didn't know much about the organization that got the money, but when its director found out about my plan, he wanted to know more about me. One day he came to visit the school that had put out the Christmas bucket. While he was there, he looked me up, thanked me and then gave me a certificate of appreciation. It was all pretty cool feeling like I'd made something good happen. I loved the feeling of being acknowledged but I didn't think that much about it at the time.

A decade later when I decided to pursue my music career I realized it was going to cost a lot to get started. Unfortunately, I had not much money and no rich friends, but I started looking around for connections I had made along the way. Finally I went to the director of that charity I'd helped out so long ago. Turned out he remembered me and that little quarter bucket at the end of the lunch line. He didn't know anything about the music business, so he introduced me to another man. This one happened to own a chain of 20 music stores around New England. One thing led to another and I convinced the music man to loan me the sound system we needed for Recycled Percussion. He was so impressed that he went on to invest $12,000 in my band to make our first live music DVD. We shipped that video everywhere we could and it became so popular it opened doors all over the country. That was our invitation to begin a successful series of tours that took my band around the world. That touring continues to this day.

Oh, and the lunch money collection I started way back then has been going ever since, too. And it's grown, spreading to lots of schools. Now they call it the Santa Fund and it's raised tens of thousands of dollars for needy kids. I sometimes wonder what difference that has made in some lives, what doors it has opened up, what paths it has created.

I guess it's pretty amazing what 25 cents can do.

Every Path Starts Somewhere

They say the entire universe started about 14 billion years ago with one Big Bang. That's a lot to take in—*everything* appearing out of *one* thing that just goes *pop* and, like some giant piñata getting whacked, all of time and space spills out. And here we are on our little planet still picking up toys and candy and bits of colored paper.

Well, if you think that's a hard act to follow, the latest theory of the universe is the Big Bang Times Infinity. Literally.

According to this idea, called the Multi-verse Theory, there are an infinite number of universes out there, each one based on what would have happened if some little thing happened differently. For example, if the Big Bang was just a little bit hotter then all the stuff in the universe would have just turned to carbon gas, like a gigantic fart, and spread out until it basically cooled into nothing. If the Big Bang was just a little cooler, it would have spewed out into chunks that would eventually run out of speed and gravity would suck them all together into a black hole or something.

I may not have all my facts completely straight here, but basically, according to this view of reality, just about anything is true somewhere. Somewhere there's a whole universe made of cheese. That's not a joke, it's a scientific theory.

So there are an endless number of other possible universes. We just happen to live in the one with Miley Cyrus on YouTube and a Dunkin' Donuts on every corner.

I'm not sure how much thought that deserves, but it does remind me of something I know is true.

The choices you make at every point in your life are way more powerful than you realize. They literally change your future. In the Talking Heads song "Once in a Lifetime" band leader David Byrne sings, "You may ask yourself; 'How did I get here?'"

That's a very good question. That's one of the most important questions you *can* ask yourself. Because if you just get a little sense of how your choices led you to where you are now, you have your finger on the kind of power it took to set off the Big Bang. The power to understand the past may not give you the power to see the future clearly, but it can save you from repeating mistakes. It can allow you to make choices that can put you lightyears ahead of where you'd wind up if you just keep wandering around in the darkness. Every decision you make is a new beginning—call it a Little Bang—that keeps on going and growing forever. Every decision you make creates a whole new universe of possibility.

If you don't believe me, you should look back and imagine what might have happened if just one little thing was different. It can shake up your world, just thinking about it.

When I was going to school, I had a hard time paying attention. I either got restless and wanted to be somewhere else or I wanted to take a nap. I had one math teacher who told me something I've never forgotten, and it had nothing to do with Algebra. He said it's OK to ignore all the classes that bore me to tears but to never fall asleep in History class.

Hmm.

There's an old saying that goes, "He who does not learn from history is doomed to repeat it." I figured that was what he was talking about so I heard him but I didn't really get it at the time. Later on, when I started to pull my own life together and to dig into other people's lives I realized that every life story shares the same threads. Everyone has those events in their lives that change things forever and those events tend to look a lot alike.

Shit happens and some are prepared when it does

while some aren't and that makes all the difference. The way to be prepared is to know where you've been and how you got where you are.

If you don't know where you've been there's no way you can know where you are going.

Seems simple when you put it like that, but let me tell you, you could write a book on just that sentence.

If you always wanted a super power, you probably had to choose between being able to fly, being invisible and being super strong. Here's a super power you can actually have. It's not as flashy as a comic book and you don't get to wear a cape. Study your past, the paths you took and where they got you and you get powerful. You find the patterns that beat you up, the way that opportunities happen. You learn that good choices pay dividends and bad ones cost you for a long time.

It sounds simple, but I'm here to tell you that almost no one bothers to do this simple thing: learn from the past. Learn how every moment has its paths, realize that every decision you make is choosing a path. You can learn from the paths you've already taken in the past and can anticipate and use that for the ones to come in the future.

Every Path Has Crossroads

A crossroads is a decision point. It can be simple, like a fork in the road or way more complicated like a Chinese menu, but if you're on a path you start by controlling your speed. Sometimes you speed up to get things done, sometimes you slow down to think things over. Both of these choices serve a purpose, so you need to choose wisely. But at points along your path you come to real choices. These are moments of potential, possibilities and every single one matters. You may think the little ones don't count. Do you choose a brownie or an apple? Do you take the stairs or the elevator? The right answer is usually pretty easy, but the important thing is that you *choose*. You don't just do what other people want you to, or what your habits make you do. You choose your path. Choose right and you get a little boost. Choose wrong and if you're paying attention you still come out ahead, because you learn something. You'll know better the next time the choice appears.

Also, you realize something along the path. Going with the flow is easy, but choosing feels good. It takes some thought, and you have to make a commitment, but you get a little boost when you make even a simple choice. This is because you were designed to make choices. That's what free will is all about. When you do what you're designed to do you get a little high. You can even get hooked on it. But it's a natural high. It's good for you.

It also prepares you for the bigger, more complicated choices. The problem with the hard choices is that you are unprepared and you may just try to play it safe. Playing it safe is not a choice, it's taking cover and hiding out until the time to choose is past. You can choose the safe route or the risky route, but unless you really make a choice it's an opportunity wasted.

And opportunities don't always come around again.

You are Always on a Path

The only way to prepare for future paths and crossroads is to learn from the past.

Ask yourself that question: "How did I get here?" and really retrace the steps. You'll be amazed what you can learn, the kind of perspective you can get.

About 18 years ago my band appeared at a high school talent show. We got a write-up in the local paper. We played wherever we could until an agency discovered us in 2001. We signed a contract to play almost 200 shows a year. We landed on the cover of *USA Today*. We sent a DVD of one of our performances to one of America's biggest TV shows, "America's Got Talent." They told us no. We prepared to go back on the road. We got another call from "America's Got Talent" saying they changed their minds and wanted us to appear. We competed on national TV, made it into the final three. We wound up losing to a country singer they called the Chicken Catcher, but suddenly we had millions of fans around the country and the world. We were able to land a full-time show in Las Vegas, where we are today.

That's the history of Recycled Percussion in a single paragraph, but there are a world of lessons in each of those

I Need You To Know

I t gets better, life does. When you feel alone, when you feel that nobody in the world can understand you, or how you feel. When it seems impossible anyone could ever relate to your dark moments, or help guide you through the maze you have found yourself lost in. It gets better. Maybe it's not white picket fences and green grass; maybe it's not winning the lottery, but it gets better. Feeling negative emotion isn't always the worst thing. It keeps the checks and balances of life leveled. It assures us we are alive. It reinforces that we care and that's why we hurt. I can testify that it gets better, that a sunny day is only a few sunrises away, that you might be witness to a new you anytime. You can look forward to the unknown, even if it is scary. What's exciting about life is trying and failing, trying and achieving, trying and learning, exploring how you ready yourself and function in the challenges you are faced with. The last thing you are is alone. We're all in it together. You are just like everyone else, trying to identify a purpose that makes you feel happy on the inside. That's what makes life a romantic journey through heartache and celebration. Create that change within yourself to power you through this long journey. You have been placed here to explore. Do it knowing that better days await you.

sentences. I could tell you what I've learned along the way, what I get from looking back, but the main lesson is simply that I didn't give up and I never just went with the flow. If I'd done that, I'd have gotten washed away a dozen times. I used every step forward or setback as an opportunity. I looked for the best choice in each crossroads and kept my eye at all times on where I wanted to go. Because I kept looking, the path opened up before me.

If you are struggling with your career plans or your entrepreneurial drive, you need to keep your eyes on the prize but also learn from where you've been. Don't repeat your mistakes if you can help it. Look for opportunities you may have missed the first time through. You've got so much valuable data in the paths you've traveled if you only take the time to look at it and put it to use.

When you are in a bad relationship, ask yourself why you got into it. Learn from the person who made that decision, the old you, but don't remain that person stuck in the negativity you've created. The new you can pack up and leave and start down a positive path.

If substances are part of your current path, be honest with yourself. Wouldn't you be faster, smarter, better able to make the changes and choices that lie ahead if you weren't poisoning yourself slowly with drugs and alcohol?

If you can't decide which way to go, look back at where you've been. When along your current path did you feel like you were going places? You can't go back. That path doesn't exist anymore and you can't walk it any more than you can step in the same river twice. The water is always different, time changes everything, but the patterns remain. Figure out what you were doing right, the direction that was taking you where you want to go. That's your compass. Start where you are and start doing those things again. Find that direction and get back on the path. Start taking every crossroads as an opportunity to recover your direction and momentum.

Create New Paths

The way to make your own path is to make your own crossroads. The confidence you earn from traveling the paths you chose can give you the ability to take on new challenges and even more risk. Soon you aren't just looking for decision points, you are making them. When you see someone who seems to be able to get from point A to point C without going through point B it may look like magic, but you are really just looking at someone who understands paths.

I spend a lot of my life flying on airplanes. Like most people I sometime just want to put on my headphones and keep my head low until I reach my destination. I know that the person sitting next to me might be doing the same thing. Every now and then something happens. You offer your seat to someone so a family can sit together and suddenly the ride changes. When you sit back down, you look at people differently. You wake up, briefly, to the possibilities all around you and that may be what it takes to get you to open up, talk to your seatmate and discover someone who can change your life for the better or inspire you in some way.

I remember reading about a rich executive of a major company who always took the time to ask the people he sat next to on a plane at least a few questions. He always wanted to know who they were and where they were from—right down to their address. He'd also ask them for their birthday date. He said it was just a habit he had adopted, a way to make his plane flights meaningful, but he would always send them a card on their birthday. Just imagine what it was like to get a birthday card, out of the blue, from someone you barely know. It would sure get your attention. Who knows how many doors he opened with those simple birthday cards. Who knows how many lives were changed by that simple act.

That was a man who knew how to make his own crossroads.

So, from the Road Less Traveled to the Highway to Hell, our decisions determine our paths. It's sentimental to think of the past as a bunch of memories, like a scrapbook, but it's actually a roadmap, a set of directions on how to get to where you really want to go. The paths you have taken have brought you to where you are today, ready to set out on the adventure of your life, so there are no regrets.

Understanding Paths is like having a personal GPS that can set your course to any destination.

And remember that the path never really ends. There's no ETA. The itinerary of your path is your life from birth to death and there's no telling what the effects might be. When you are no longer traveling your path, you have still blazed a trail for others to follow and carry on where you left off.

Use the perspective you've gained from the paths you've traveled and fix your eye on your Legacy and nothing can stand in your way for long.

Actions

1. Think of two or three of the most important events of your life and answer these questions:
    a. What are the most important decision(s) you made that got you there?
    b. What can you learn from those choices that might help you with a current decision?
2. Think of at least one way that you can create more crossroads in your life, starting tomorrow. What can you do every day that will open up new possibilities for your future?

Strategies

(Got a plan? A crazy idea? A way to fix the world?
Write that shit down and do it!)

"An architect's most useful tools are an eraser at the drafting board and a wrecking bar at the site."

—Frank Lloyd Wright

Meganode 3 — The Architect

MY AVERAGE SCORE IN CANDLEPIN BOWLING was 108. I was the youngest regular at Boutwell's Bowling Center in Concord, New Hampshire, and I was probably the only adult who wasn't drinking beer and slipping out back for a smoke between sets. With my tattoos, rock 'n' roll haircut and technicolor clothes I guess I stood out in the crowd of families dressed in Dockers, pressed jeans and NASCAR shirts, but these were my people. This was where I belonged. This bowling alley had saved my life.

A year before, in 1996, I had been at the Olympic Summer Games in Atlanta. I'd spent a hot day watching field hockey and walking around the sun-baked streets of the Capitol of the South. Lying in my hotel bed, a bit worn out, I had a sudden feeling of anxiety. Nothing too weird at first, but it didn't start to go away, like most moods. Instead it revved up like a stock car engine and turned into a feeling of total white hot fear. I didn't know what was happening to me, but I knew what I thought. I thought I was going to die. The thought was terrifying.

I crawled into the shower, thinking it would cool me off, but it was 20 minutes before I was myself again. All

I could think was, "What the fuck?" Two weeks later the experience was pretty much forgotten. I'd chalked it up to a heat stroke. Put it behind me.

Then it happened again. And again.

And as the weeks went by these spells, that I now knew to be panic attacks, became so common that just the thought that I *might* get one was enough to trigger a new one. I'm an extrovert, an outgoing kid, but I was afraid to leave the house, scared it would happen in public or cause danger to myself or someone else. I slumped into serious depression. I was unable to leave my apartment except to see doctors who began prescribing me a menu of drugs, antidepressants, anti-anxiety drugs, God knows what. My fear of dying was still there, but worse was the very real fear of losing everything else, my relationships, my family, my girlfriend and my job.

The drugs weren't doing the trick. I knew I had to try something on my own, break out of this prison of fear. My apartment was just a block from a bowling alley so I walked down and checked it out. This was not "big ball" bowling like in the Big Lebowski. This was pure New England candlepin. I bowled a string and did a quick head check. No panic. So far, so good. The place was dim, calm and predictable. People were so focused in their little groups, with just occasional bursts of excitement over a strike or when someone cleaned up a tough spare. Even the sounds of the balls hitting the tall wooden pins was muffled and soothing.

I didn't just become a regular, I joined a league. I bowled for hours on end, improving my score, but every day I was also making tiny steps out of my depression and fear. That bowling alley was a miniature world that was within my control. It gave me a place where I could work through my anxieties, move beyond them, find my way back to normal.

Normal for me is not normal for everyone. In school, I'd been coded as hyperactive at 8. Doctors wanted to put me on Ritalin but my parents refused. I've got it under more control now, but I'm ADD to this day. I won't take the drugs. It's not for everyone, I know. Medicine has done a lot of good, I'm sure, but I prefer to find my own ways of controlling my moods, finding my focus. And doing so has taught me that we have more power than we know. I needed to change, but the biggest obstacles to change are not the physical ones, they are mental.

In the darkest period of my life when I really wanted to hide, instead I reached out and tried something new. The panic I experienced robbed me of my purpose in life, my direction, left me with no idea why I was even here. Bowling showed me there was something new, another way to approach my challenges. You can find solace and inspiration in the strangest places. The world is full of opportunities like that if you are brave enough to seek them out. Find something to spark a new interest in your mind, and with it you'll find a new beginning.

The Architect

In our culture the body gets all the credit. Think about the most famous people in America and most of them are muscular sports stars, hot-looking actors from Hollywood or sexy singers from Nashville. Ask people on the street to name the most intelligent people in the world and you'll usually get the names of either politicians (who are really kind of like professional wrestlers) or writers (who are really like entertainers). Ask them to name three scientists and you'll usually get Einstein, Einstein and Einstein.

And the power of the mind isn't just about intelligence. Being super smart is a little bit like being muscle bound. It's not what you've got, it's what you do with it. The true strength of the mind is all about focus, clear thinking, rationality, sanity. There are plenty of awards for people who are the best spellers or who can answer the most trivia questions on *Jeopardy*, but it's hard to hold a contest for who is the most sane or level-headed person in the world. You may have heard people say, "There's nothing less common than common sense." I'm afraid that's true, but it's not because people don't have it, they just don't use it.

Make no mistake, the body *is* crucial. That's why there's an entire chapter devoted to it here in Legacy X (The Machine) but everything the body does, every project you build, every plan you make, it all starts somewhere else. That place is hard to put your finger on. It's in some

48

We All Have These Days . . .

headline in a show on the Las Vegas strip, I perform for a living and am fortunate enough to have fans that want to pay to see a show I have created. They want autographs and they want to be a part of what my show is, even if for a moment. Given this blessing of a lifestyle I still have the same bad days as the guy that gets up and sits in an office all day while looking out the window daydreaming of a life that doesn't resemble the one he is living. No matter if we are rich, poor, white, black, young or old we all are met with our own respective challenges that affect our lives. I have days where I wonder to myself if I am in fact happy. I have days where I wonder if I can do better, how I can make myself happier, days where I feel like the world is coming down on me. From the outside my life would seem amazing and to me it is in many ways. However this doesn't make me invisible to negativity. I am human just like the guy in the office; I have the same crushing blows that attack me from time to time. When this happens, I think about how lucky I am to be alive, truly alive, alive with the free choice to live life on my terms, the very same choices you have. How lucky we are to not be living on the streets, to be born in an amazing country, to have the choices we have, and to be the ones in control of our emotions. We are so lucky, all of us are, and most of the time we don't even realize it. We put ourselves in positions that disguise the happiness we control. We all have the bad days and we all have the same choices to make them good days. The choice is yours.

invisible control room where you make the decisions and deal with the consequences of your decisions and figure out ways to make better decisions. It's not always calm in that room. It's like air traffic control. The stakes are high and sometimes there's just too much going on. Things don't always make sense the way we'd like them to.

Who are You?

People call it your self, or maybe your soul. It's the "I" that you use when you talk about yourself, but does that answer the question or just make it more complicated. I mean, really, who the fuck are you?

Maybe the simplest way to answer that question is to look at what you do, or what you do with what you've got. That's what most people say when asked "Who are you?" If you dig ditches, you answer, "I'm a ditch digger." If you take care of sick people, you say "I'm a nurse."

But what if what you do isn't what you really want to do? What if your goals are much, much bigger than your present job? I think the real answer to the question "who am I" is that I am the designer of my life. The body is the builder, but I am the Architect. And that's what you are too. You are imagining the life you want to lead, deciding what you can achieve, creating the blueprints and giving instructions to make your ultimate plans into realities. If you don't want to be your own designer, too bad. No one else can do it for you, though people can sure fuck up your life if you let them.

In fact, if you don't take control, you are really just letting someone else do it. Picture that in a car. You're behind the wheel but you let someone tell you where to go, when to brake, where to pull over. It's not just stupid, it's dangerous.

The Architect of your own life—that's an incredibly powerful position to be in. Especially since you've got your body pretty much at your control, ready to do your bidding, right? In your dreams. If only it was that easy. Apparently there's some disconnect somewhere. The message gets garbled. The body does whatever it feels like. The mind goes on vacations.

I talk to people all the time who seem to have just settled for whatever has happened to them, and that's pretty much how they view their lives—like something that happened to them. The world is a place they were strolling through until somewhere along the line they got stuck. And now that their situation has gotten complicated they just give up. They accept mediocrity. They think, "Shit, it's not that bad. At least we've got wi-fi and HBO. And I hear the next season of *Game of Thrones* is going to kick ass."

Why can't they see the opportunity they have? Why isn't it crystal clear to them that you don't get given the kind of potential that they possess without a real purpose, a real mission? It's basically like getting a wad of cash and using it as toilet paper or a hunk of pure gold and using it as a paperweight. It's like taking that red ping pong ball they got out of the swimming pool of life and turning it into a clown nose. It's like they are mistaking that butterfly feeling they had in their stomachs when they first got a glimpse of their Legacy for indigestion. So they pop some antacid pills and take a nap.

Wake up the Architect

Something is screwed up. The Architect must have passed out somewhere along the line. The builders are just nailing shit together with no plan.

You gotta wake the Architect up and head back to the drawing board with a sharp pencil and a fresh eraser.

Have you ever been in love? I hope so. You've got to know that feeling that here's a person you'd do anything for, go to any lengths to be with. You can't stop thinking about that person day and night. When you are apart, you want to get together. When you are together you want to get closer. Hold that thought, remember that feeling for a second. That's your clue.

Now, go somewhere you can be alone, completely alone. Bring nothing but a pad of paper and a pencil (and yeah, make sure you have an eraser). Forget about everything that nags your mind for awhile. Set aside your friends and families, forget about what everyone else expects of you, even your job. Especially your job. This is about you waking up the Architect.

Now try to remember the things you always wanted to accomplish, no matter how crazy or unlikely. Write down everything you can think of that would make you proud to be a part of, happy to be working towards, excited to get up in the morning and pursue every day. If you start to think it's ridiculous, that's no reason to stop. That probably means you're getting close. Don't judge, just dream or imagine what your perfect world would be like, what you would be doing in it. What are the things you wouldn't mind sacrificing for, the things you could defend with your life?

At some point in this exercise, see if you get a glimpse of that clue, start to feel those butterflies that you know from that last time you were in love. That's like a Geiger counter clicking away, helping you find your Legacy. Don't give up, because it's there somewhere.

Once you find it it may take a while to clear out the cobwebs. It may have been hidden there for years, decades, but your Legacy never gets old.

It may come back to you little bits at a time—things you set aside that you intended to get back to.

My Fantastic Idea

Back when I was 25 years old I remember I had a vision. I knew it was a fantastic idea and I wanted to make it happen.

I loved racing, and I imagined a high-stakes road race that took place over 24 hours with the winning driver receiving a million dollar prize. But it wasn't just a race. It was also a scavenger hunt with a series of clues along the way that led the drivers to the final destination where the prize was hidden. I came up with a name, "Mission 24" and a complete plan. I had logos designed. I was ready to rock 'n' roll. I'd even spent about $15,000 of my earnings and savings to create the fliers and advertising to promote the event. That bought a pallet full of boxes of printed materials.

At the last minute, my legal counsel told me we'd hit a roadblock. We couldn't find an insurance company to grant a policy for the event. We had a great plan but lost on a technicality. I took it pretty hard, but I kept those boxes of handouts for three years. I kept them as a reminder of the passion I felt and as motivation to never allow roadblocks to stop me again.

I really loved that idea. It gives me butterflies. Believe it or not, I think it may still happen.

One word of caution. The down side of putting your plans on hold and then forgetting them, is that you lose something essential. You lose hope. You put plans on the back burner long enough and they boil away to nothing. This is the formula for depression. It's that gnawing anxiety that something isn't right, that you've lost something for good.

Not all depression and anxiety comes from this. Sometimes it's chemical, something you just got at birth. But don't just accept mental states that hold you back. That's how people who have given up behave. Fight back, talk to experts. Try something new, the way I tried bowling. Some people need medication, but don't settle for feeling better. That's not what it's all about, just feeling better. You are going for the gold, the greatest feeling in the world. The knowledge that you are working toward your true calling in life, the reason you exist.

Think of what you spend your time on. Watching TV for most of your non-working day, living your life through fictional characters on a big screen or worse on a tiny screen (I'm talking about you, Facebook) is really pathetic if you think about it. And even if you aren't *thinking* about it, part of you knows that. It's enough to depress anyone, to watch a life being wasted. And if the person watching you waste your life is *you*, then that might explain why your mental health is suffering.

Another thing people do to compensate for a sense of challenge, mission and purpose is to go out and shop. Shopping is basically just a drug. It makes you feel good while it clogs up your life. It hides your insecurities while making them worse, because gradually you believe that your worth is dictated by what you own, not who you are. You find you have stronger emotional attachments to the things you own than to the people you say you love. That's a problem.

Try going around your home with a pad of fluorescent sticky notes and put one on every single object that you know you could live without. Write on those notes how much money you spent on each item. Add it up. What could you have bought with that money? Maybe you could have paid for a year of business school so you could start that company you have in the back of your mind. Maybe you could have paid to create a Web site to sell the handcrafts you've always wanted to make, or just paid for a healthy diet and a gym membership.

Ask yourself, what were you thinking? Your plans disappear in drips and drops, just like the money you waste on booze or drugs. Cigarettes are four dollars a pack. A pack a day for 15 years is $21,000. Twenty-one-thousand-fucking dollars that you spent on nothing but bodily harm, bad breath and an early death.

No wonder you're depressed.

Starting Over

It's time to hit the reset button. Start a new building plan.

Gaining the kind of focus and perspective that the Architect needs isn't something you can easily get from a book. We're talking about reprogramming your central processing unit. But there are some tricks that can get you out of a rut or stop the needle from skipping on the vinyl record album.

Richard Carlson, who wrote the self-help book *Don't Sweat the Small Stuff*, offers about 100 techniques. One of the simplest is this. Become an Early Riser. If you want a new perspective on life, get up at least an hour before you really have to start getting ready for your day. Use that time to plan the day out, or to pray and meditate if that's your thing, or to practice your ukulele. You can pretty much guarantee that it will be the least interrupted hour in your entire day so take advantage of it. Give it a month and see if it works for you.

The bottom line is that you've opened up something new, a space you can use. You've stopped going with the flow. It's called taking control of your life.

Identify something you do all the time that's not helpful and stop it. Just stop. If you swear you can't stop smoking to save your life (which it very well might) then do it for a different reason. Do it just to see what will happen. Make up your mind to stop right now and get a note pad or a mini recorder and simply take notes on what happens to you. How you deal with each urge for a cigarette. Remember, it's an experiment, not an intervention. All you are promising to do is go as long as you can without smoking and record how you feel, how you cope with the feelings, what are your excuses when (if) you decide to give up. You may find out that you never smoke again, you may have a butt hanging out of your mouth ten minutes later, but if you didn't write anything down or record your thoughts, then you are just cheating. Start over.

If you are one of those people who can't let others get a word in, commit to listening to other people speak and don't interrupt them or finish their sentences. Then count to five before you talk.

If you are quiet and don't like to speak up, promise yourself that for an entire day you will say whatever comes into your head in a loud clear voice. If you sound like a robot and people start to worry about you, tell them about what you are doing in a loud clear voice. It will blow their minds. They will start to look at you differently.

You'll start to look at yourself differently. Because you'll be different.

You may be comfortable as a leader or you may not, but you can't turn down the job. You are the boss of your company, so the more you know about leadership, the better you will do. The Architect is your model of a leader. It's the leader within you.

One of the first things about being a leader is to recognize leadership in others whenever you see it. Learn to speak Architect to Architect with other people and you'll find that people respond. The boss of you is talking to the boss of them. That's when things happen. Your enthusiasm can awaken the plans of others. When you identify a leader within your circle of partners, you see it for the opportunity that it is. Awakening the Architect within you and discovering the Architects around you is fundamental to achieving your Legacy.

The world is changed by people willing to change themselves. When you change the world by taking control of your own life you become a leader and your strength will benefit others in their own work. The world is changed one person at a time and each one of us has to lead the way.

The Architect is the leader you've been looking for and that's where all your plans begin.

Actions

1. Spend one week doing things differently. Get up an hour early. Change a habit. Keep at it no matter what the results are, starting over every day and learning from what happens.

2. To wake up your Architect, start seeking out the Architect in your friends and relations. Talk to the part of them that is designing the future, not living in the past. Make friends with that part of your friends and you will soon be surrounded by other people working on their Legacies.

Strategies

(Got a plan? A crazy idea? A way to fix the world?
Write that shit down and do it!)

"Your body is the only place
you have to live."

—The late, great Jim Rohn, motivational speaker

Meganode 4 — The Machine

I'M COOKING EGG WHITES on a gas barbecue grill in an old warehouse. Red paint chips off the walls and the clang of heat pipes and the scurrying of rats is drowned out by a boom box playing Led Zeppelin at full volume. I scrape the last bite of egg into my mouth, turn off the music, pack my towel and a small suitcase and push through the heavy door out into a cold New Hampshire morning.

Back in 2000 I found myself thumbing through the want ads in the *Manchester Union Leader* newspaper, looking for a place to live. I already had a $4,000-a-month apartment in Midtown Manhattan and was tooling around in a Lotus Elise (a real step up from that beat up old Ford Escort with the rock 'n' roll bumper stickers). Now I was looking for something different. It's surprisingly hard to find a place to live that has a bathroom but no shower, no kitchen and no air conditioning, but I found it. Good thing, too, because that apartment got me in the best shape of my life.

It was a 5,000-square-foot empty space in one of Manchester's old mill buildings. It was pretty minimalistic, but I put up a zip line from one wall to the other, just for fun, and I slept on a giant bean bag with a comforter. I'd bought a $69 Weber propane grill for cooking (probably in violation of a dozen city codes) so my options for meals were pretty slim, mostly scrambled eggs and chicken. The simple diet helped keep me slim, too.

I'd made the decision to strip my life down to the things I really needed: my phone, my car, my computer and my gym membership. With no AC or bath, and being a healthy young aspiring rock star, I had to visit the gym every morning to get a shower. It was all part of the plan.

I was already in pretty good shape, but it wasn't because I loved going to the gym. I had to force myself like anyone else. I couldn't risk letting my passion go stale, or allow myself to come up with excuses. I was good at making excuses. I'd figured that much out about myself, so I had to take a radical approach. I knew that I had to make it a necessity. I even considered renting a gym locker so that every evening I could leave my wallet there, forcing me to come back the next morning.

But the shower plan worked. By making the gym a necessity, going there every day became an operating principle in my life. It reinforced my conviction that it was imperative for me to always be in my very best shape. To succeed at anything, you've got to acknowledge your weaknesses and plan how to combat them. I love that scene in the movie *Fight Club* where Brad Pitt points at a poster of some male models in a subway car. He asks are we getting in shape to look like that or to become soldiers.

My daily workout is like a little bootcamp every day.

Sometimes people ask me, "Are you training for something special." I tell them "I'm training for life."

The world throws all kinds of shit at you when you try to get in shape. So ask yourself, are you just working out to look like a model, or are you working out to become a soldier? Just know that you're going to have to fight for the things that are most important to your life and your Legacy.

Overhauling and Fine Tuning

The Machine is fundamental, essential, precious and powerful. If you are trying to build a Legacy without taking care of and fine-tuning the machine then you are building castles in the air. You've got no foundation and no juice.

The Machine is your body and all of the stuff you carry around and the things you put inside it, the fuel you use, the care you take minus the damage you inflict. There's nothing more important. It's the vehicle that takes you to every place you want to go. It's the system that achieves all the other goals. Strength flows out of this system like horsepower from a well-tuned engine. That's if you take care of it. If you don't take care or it or you gunk it up with substances, overeating, sitting on your ass, then you sure as shit won't get the benefits.

Sure, it's a little bit like a car. You may need to tune things up or you may need a complete overhaul. But there the comparison ends. You can buy a new car, you only get one body.

Look over the list of things you most want to achieve and ask yourself if accomplishing and/or enjoying every single one of those things isn't benefitted by taking care of your Machine. Small improvements can make a huge difference because we're talking about the long haul, here. This is the category that adds momentum and power to every other one.

And it's really not just about your body, because the things you learn about yourself from getting in shape are just as important, maybe even more important than the benefits to your body. Signals from your body, and how you react to them, are the most basic intelligence you possess, your instincts, your reflexes. Your brain is part of your Machine. If you want a healthy brain, take care of the rest of the package.

If you like to flex your muscles in front of a mirror, fine, but don't be confused. What this is *not* about is what you look like, it's not about what people think about you, but it is about what you think about yourself and your abilities, your confidence and your situational awareness.

It's not important you be a world class athlete, a Mr. or Ms. Olympian, unless that's your goal. It's not that you can never eat a donut. It's about taking care of the part of you that takes care of business. It's about having a physical basis for your convictions. If you can't take care of the physical stuff, it doesn't speak well for your ability to handle anything else. That said, here are two of my own personal convictions, rules that I live by.

1. I believe, hell, I *know*, physical fitness is essential to building a Legacy.
2. I have a zero tolerance policy for substances: drugs, alcohol, or any shit that makes you feel good at the expense of your physical well being or your mental integrity.

Better than the new iPhone

Your Machine is an awesome tool so why would you put anything in it to fuck it up? If you've already run your Machine down or gunked it up, you have one great thing going for you. It's so awesome that if you just stop abusing it, it can usually return to full power in a matter of weeks. Usually. And even if you've done permanent damage, you can work around it once you get serious. That's how great it is.

In fact, the human body is an absolute miracle. It's like the coolest piece of technology ever made, able to do just about anything, go anywhere, it communicates clearly and understands all voice commands. It never needs new batteries and it automatically recharges every night. It's packed with the very best apps and the more you use it the smarter, stronger and more fun it becomes. It's compatible with all your other devices, able to tolerate extreme weather and dangerous situations and if you drop it or smash it up it can usually repair itself. If it does get permanently damaged, it's able to reallocate resources to compensate. It solves its own problems and has enough bandwidth and processing speed to run an international corporation or to manage a family budget. It even can reproduce itself. The only reason you don't wet your pants wishing you could have one is that you already do, but the chances are you don't even think about it. Or you just take it for granted.

The human ear can detect a mosquito buzzing three feet away or hear a baby crying in an upstairs bedroom. It can recognize a single voice from a million different ones. It can tell if that voice is happy or pissed off and a dozen different moods in between. The human eye can see a fastball pitch and tell the muscles in the arm to start to aim for a specific spot somewhere in the air where a ball is most likely to be ¼ second after the decision is made to swing.

Properly trained, human legs can run about 25 miles per hour (Usain Bolt can run 28 mph). The highest a person can jump straight up is about two feet, but Cuban athlete Javier Sotomayer cleared an 8 foot and a quarter inch high bar to set a world record. Look at your ceiling (probably about seven feet high) and imagine how you could jump over that. Drumming is something I know a thing or two about. A Canadian guy named Tom Grosset has been recorded as drumming 1,208 beats in a minute. That's more than 20 per second. Not bad.

And it's not just about extremes. Or famous athletes. You do miracles every day with your machine.

Human hands can thread a needle, hammer a nail and make a soufflé. They can play "Flight of the Bumblebee" on a violin or perform a quadruple bypass. You can sense the heat of a sick kid's forehead or you can enjoy the touch of skin that causes a different kind of heat. That's a sensitive device.

There's pain, too, but even that is usually a good thing. It tells you when you've had enough or when you've done something wrong. Or it gives you something to overcome, to make you strong in a different way.

Something's Wrong

But when pain and suffering teach people nothing, there's something seriously wrong. The fact that Americans can't stop stuffing their mouths isn't just making some funny videos about Walmart people, it's costing everyone serious bucks. A study by the United States Centers for Disease Control and Prevention estimates that obesity costs the country about $147 billion per year. The CDC says that childhood obesity has doubled in little children and tripled in teens in the last 30 years. Thousands of overweight teens are getting treated for high blood pressure and diabetes.

These aren't fat cigar smoking, martini drinking, CEOs. We're talking about kids. It's fucking crazy.

When it comes to diet, like anything, you start with what you actually need. If you were a soldier and had a limited supply of food you'd be aware of every calorie you ate, because it would be a calorie you wouldn't have later. If you have to carry a 60-pound pack of supplies, then you need more calories. But if you are a teacher or a business person and you are carrying around 30 extra pounds of body fat, then you need fewer calories. Why this confuses people is a mystery to me, but that's the way it is. We confuse food with love or with comfort, when it's really fuel. The fact that it gives pleasure is part of the confusion. Nothing wrong with the joy of a great steak or the taste of an excellent dessert, but when something that gives pleasure starts to cause pain—like maybe a bad case of sciatica from carrying around a huge gut—or sickness like heart disease and cancer, and you still can't stop eating, you know there was already something sick going on.

There's nothing wrong with feeling good, especially when you get that feeling from something you accomplish or maybe from being with loved ones or friends, maybe from exploring the world. But when the pleasure comes with no effort from a bottle or a pill or a puff of weed, any sane person should wonder if there's something fishy going on. Chemicals that make you feel very good also have the power to make you feel very bad. And the easy

Do Yourself a Favor

Commit to making this a good week, start your Monday with energy, eat a little better, make a little more time for things you like, do *one* thing you have been putting off and do *one* thing for your community no matter how small! It's all really that simple and that easy. But it's impossible unless you do it. I need you to be *brave* as you face challenges and changes. *Many* of you are tackling big changes in life, all positive, long-term, not-going-to-be-easy changes, but *you will be brave.* You won't fail this time. This time will be different. Go get em'. Win.

fix of a drug is just simply too easy. Your body eventually gets the message. Why work for my pleasure when I can get it for "free?"

So what do you lose when you start to feed your machine substances? Well the first thing to suffer is the drive to find that pleasure in constructive ways. You don't really need those adventures. Good friends become secondary to friends who share your habits. Friends who don't partake can actually start to get on your nerves. They seem so judgmental. And why develop your abilities or explore nature when you can find the same pleasure sitting on the sofa watching TV with the sound off and the stereo blasting?

I'm not giving you a D.A.R.E. lecture. This isn't some bullshit "Just Say No" speech. I've been in the music business for 20 years and I've kept my priorities straight which are my goals and my Legacy. Anything else has to go. And though I've managed to avoid getting sucked into all this, trust me—I've seen it all.

And just because it's legal doesn't mean that alcohol isn't every bit as destructive as any drug. Binge drinking at college used to be news. Campus cops and administrations would get worked up and crack down from time to time. Now it's just another night in the dorm. No one takes much notice except when someone dies.

And lots of people are dying. In 2010, 38 percent more Americans got ambulance rides to emergency rooms to be treated for alcohol poisoning than ten years earlier. Binge drinking isn't just a college fad. A lot of those people trying to kill themselves with booze call themselves "grown ups." There's something seriously fucked up going on, obviously, and it's a bigger problem than any one person can handle, but you *can* handle one part of the problem, the part closest to you, the part that affects you the most. You can control *you*.

The Good News

And the good news is that if you are willing to stay out of that shit, you have many advantages. When your drinking friends are hung over, sleeping in after a night of hard partying, you are up early working on your mission. When your druggie friends are out spending $60 on a tiny bag of weed or God-knows-what on some hard drugs for pipe dreams, you are saving your money to roll into an investment on cool real plans for your future.

You could say that I depend on a substance, too. My high comes from the substance of my goals. I score every time I get a step closer to my Legacy. The difference is that my substance is free and real and healthy and you can get the same fix without having to waste your money, your life and your self respect on drugs and alcohol.

Getting off those phony substances should happen immediately, *Today*. Making fitness an integral part of your life should happen now, too. You don't have to wait until you get a gym membership or sign up for a diet plan to commit to healthy living and start living it out. Getting in maximum shape comes in smaller doses over time. But that's really OK, because every little bit can make a big difference. You can leverage just a little more strength or stamina just the same way you gain compound interest on an investment. It adds up, slowly at first, then at some point you look back and go, "Wow. How did that happen?"

It's different for everyone, but we all can benefit.

After all, not all machines are created equal. Some come off the factory floor with defects, some do get damaged beyond repair. Life isn't fair in what it deals out, but you play the hand you've been dealt. It takes less than you think to be great, to do great work and make a difference.

A journalist named Jean-Dominique Bauby was the editor of *Elle* magazine in France. He was living a high life, hanging out with models and sophisticates when he had a massive stroke, woke up in the hospital and eventually realized he was completely paralyzed. Completely except for one thing. He could blink his left eye. He eventually worked out a code with his blinks and communicated it to a nurse. Soon he was writing every night in his mind, and then the next day he would "transcribe" his words to the nurse by blinking. He wrote a book about his life, *The Diving Bell and the Butterfly*, using that system. It was a best seller for years and has sold millions of copies, and was made into a movie.

That book turned out to be his Legacy.

It doesn't take much, just a mission and a will to keep going.

When NASA sent the Voyager 1 into space it had less computing power than your digital watch, but it's still out there, sending back signals, just about to leave our solar system, eleven billion miles and 36 years after it was launched. Back in 1990, when it was about four billion miles away, science writer Carl Sagan asked NASA to turn it's camera back for one last shot of the Earth. Our planet looked like a pale blue pixel in the darkness of space. Google "pale blue dot" if you want to see the picture.

So you can do a lot with a little if you know what you're doing and if you are willing to get creative. Or even if you aren't particularly creative, think of it like this. The way to take the lead isn't to run faster than everyone all the time. That can wear you out, but what if you just take an extra few steps in the right direction every day? Just lots of little steps over a long period of time with a sense of direction will absolutely separate you from the rest of the pack. That's true in fitness, in business, in art. And it makes you better and smarter, too. That old saying "practice makes perfect," may be a little optimistic, but it sure as hell makes you better.

A Healthy Machine is Magnetic

It starts with a sense of self respect. You aren't getting

ahead to leave others behind. You are doing it because you have places to go.

And treating yourself with respect will cause other people to do the same. If you look like you don't give a shit about yourself, then that's pretty much how other people will feel about you as well.

It's not all physical, either. "A healthy mind in a healthy body," used to be the formula for success. One supports the other and together they are unbeatable. Ask the runners who were able to stop taking antidepressants when they started putting in miles every day. Ask me. I used to struggle with depression and anxiety. Exercise is the one proven drug-free remedy. I'm living proof.

And it contributes to your financial success as well. Healthy people do better in business. They inspire confidence. People like to be around other people who are in shape. It inspires them. Health can be contagious just like sickness can, and people want to get close to it, it's a bug that people want to catch. Healthy people and successful people are magnetic.

Here's an unscientific survey you can conduct yourself. It's something I notice every time I go to the gym. Check the parking lot of a fitness center. Add up in your mind the approximate retail value of the first 10 cars you see. Now do the same thing at a grocery store, or an apartment building or just about anywhere and you'll notice that the people who go to the gym tend to be doing pretty well. I'm not saying money is the most important thing, but it's an indication that people who take care of themselves also are the people who succeed in accomplishing their goals in life, both health wise and financially.

Your body is raw power, just waiting for you to tap it, use it, build things with it, enjoy it.

The question is not should you get fit. It's how can you possibly justify *not* taking the best possible care of your machine. How can you waste that power?

Like Spider-Man says, with great power comes great responsibility. You have to take responsibility for your own machine, keep it in shape, use it for good work, to get to where you need to be, not to waste time and get bogged down in shit you don't need.

What Do You Need?

If you need any proof that material possessions can be as addictive as heroin, just watch the TV show *Hoarders*. Those may be extreme examples, but explain why most two-car garages have no room left for cars, or why the storage industry is booming so much that now they will drop off a storage shed at your home, let you fill it up and then drive it away. And you know that most of those units could be dropped in the ocean and the owners of all that crap would never miss a thing.

How much do you really need? What kind of things help you. What things slow you down?

Things are good. You want things that help you work, make life fun and interesting, open up the world to you. What you don't want is things that clutter up your life, get in your way.

Do an inventory of the things in your life and put each one to the test: does this make me a better person, does it make me happy, does it make me more powerful to have? If you can't answer absolutely yes to at least one of those questions, either sell it, put it in a trash bag or ship it to the Salvation Army.

Too many things make us into a thing. And you are not a thing. An old scientist named R. Buckminster Fuller (he invented the geodesic dome and a bunch of other future stuff back in the 1960s) once said, "I seem to be a verb." Get it? Not a noun, but a verb. Not a thing, but an action. Bob Dylan sang, "He who is not busy being born is busy dying." Amen to that.

You get loaded up with things that don't help you to grow and you start to die. Simple as that.

That goes for what you put in your body, too. You can find tons of diet advice, but in the end it doesn't really matter what plan you use, just don't become a thing, remain a verb. Stay active and eat intentionally, not by habit. Eat stuff that makes you strong and eat stuff that you enjoy and you'll be fine. But don't eat to try to make yourself happy. That's a recipe for being fat, sad and dead.

The path to Legacy X is to equip your machine like a

soldier. A soldier only carries the thing he or she needs to survive and to accomplish the mission. Look for the chapter on Paths in this book and see why you need to be ready to take advantage of every situation. You don't know when an opportunity will arise, and the one you miss could be the most important one in your life. Being fit, traveling light, a healthy mind and body will equip you to be on guard, even in random moments.

Being a soldier fighting for your Legacy requires complete commitment to your own physical health and the systematic removal of all blocks and hindrances. This includes behaviors and substances that degrade performance and material possessions that do not serve to further your goals. The things you consume have the power to consume you, If you don't watch out, the things you own end up owning you.

Where to begin? There are literally thousands of books on diet and fitness, and we've got great information on legacyX.com. If you want to do something radical, then lock your wallet at the gym each night so you've got to go get it every day, pay someone to kick your ass every morning, but come on. There are 168 hours in a week. If you can't find five of those hours, two percent of your life, to dedicate to this most basic thing, your own physical fitness, then close the book, you're done.

Actions

I'm going to make this easy for you. I already know all the excuses because I hear them all the time. Below are all your excuses and my answers, just to save some time. If I missed one send it to me at LegacyX.com and we'll come up with something tailored just for you.

Excuses not to Exercise

1. *I haven't got the time.*

   You need to give 45 minutes of positive effort out of your 16 waking hours. First place I suggest you look for the time is either watching Epic Fail videos on the Internet or sitting in front of the TV—both of which tend to be negative activities that you'd be better off without anyway.

2. *I don't have a gym.*

   No gym is required, though there's probably one within 15 minutes of anyone in the United States. If you want gym-free suggestions for getting in shape, go to LegacyX.com for a list of suggestions designed for people in all phases of fitness.

3. *My kids interfere or I've got no babysitter.*

   Most gyms have a babysitting service, but you've probably got a friend with a kid about the same age as yours. Why not take turns or maybe find some exercise you can do with the kids along. There's no better example you can set and starting them early is a great idea.

4. *I don't know how.*

   Have you heard of a little thing called the Internet? There are

endless web sites (including our own) that can offer tips on how
to put together a plan that works for you.

5. *I'm too busy because of my job.*

And yet you probably have time on the job to check your
Facebook. Take your work to the gym with you on a pad
or smart phone while you're on the stationary bike. Make
fitness part of your job. Cut your lunch break in half to run.
Understand that exercise before work will improve your
performance on the job and make you better at what you do.

6. *I hate exercising.*

That's because you don't do it. If you did, then you'd see
the benefits and you'd be insane not to work out. It's about
overcoming obstacles, not giving in to them. That's the whole
point.

Bottom line is you've probably spent more time looking for
an excuse than it would to get yourself to a gym. In other words,
"No excuses."

Excuses Not to Control Your Diet

1. *Why should I? I'll never be sexy.*

Come on. It's not about how you look, it's about having the
energy to obtain your goals. And sex is really a lot more about
energy than it is about looks anyway. Bring some healthy energy
and fitness to bed and you'll find out what "sexy" really is.

2. *But I love junk food.*

Maybe you love your cat, but that doesn't mean you have a

dozen of them. You're probably happy to have a trash can in your house, too, but that doesn't mean your house has to be full of trash.

3. *I've worked out hard today, so I'll just forget the diet.*

Sure, you took two steps forward, so you deserve to take two steps back.

4. *I'm stressed out and food relaxes me.*

I suppose already having one major cause of heart attacks is a good reason to add another one.

5. *Life is too short, so I'm going to eat what I want.*

Translated: "Life is too short, so I'm going to make it shorter."

Strategies

(Got a plan? A crazy idea? A way to fix the world?
Write that shit down and do it!)

WHO'S IN CONTROL HERE?

ONLY YOU ARE IN CONTROL OF YOU ONLY YOU ARE IN
YOU ARE IN CONTROL OF YOU ONLY YOU ARE IN CONT
ARE IN CONTROL OF YOU ONLY YOU ARE IN CONTROL
IN CONTROL OF YOU ONLY YOU ARE IN CONTROL OF
CONTROL OF YOU ONLY YOU ARE IN CONTROL OF YOU O
OF YOU ONLY YOU ARE IN CONTROL OF YOU ONLY YO
YOU ONLY YOU ARE IN CONTROL OF YOU ONLY YOU A
ONLY YOU ARE IN CONTROL OF YOU ONLY YOU ARE IN
YOU ARE IN CONTROL OF YOU ONLY YOU ARE IN CONT
ARE IN CONTROL OF YOU HIT THE RESET BUTTON ONLY
OF YOU ONLY YOU ARE IN CONTROL OF YOU ONLY YO
YOU ONLY YOU ARE IN CONTROL OF YOU ONLY YOU A
ONLY YOU ARE IN CONTROL OF YOU ONLY YOU ARE IN
YOU ARE IN CONTROL OF YOU ONLY YOU ARE IN CONT
ARE IN CONTROL OF YOU ONLY YOU ARE IN CONTROL
IN CONTROL OF YOU ONLY YOU ARE IN CONTROL OF
CONTROL OF YOU ONLY YOU ARE IN CONTROL OF YOU O
OF YOU ONLY YOU ARE IN CONTROL OF YOU ONLY YO
YOU ONLY YOU ARE IN CONTROL OF YOU ONLY YOU A
ONLY YOU ARE IN CONTROL OF YOU ONLY YOU ARE IN
YOU ARE IN CONTROL OF YOU ONLY YOU ARE IN CONT
ARE IN CONTROL OF YOU ONLY YOU ARE IN CONTROL
IN CONTROL OF YOU ONLY YOU ARE IN CONTROL OF YO
YOU ARE IN CONTROL OF YOU ONLY YOU ARE IN CONT
ARE IN CONTROL OF YOU ONLY YOU ARE IN CONTROL O
CONTROL OF YOU ONLY YOU ARE IN CONTROL OF YOU O
OF YOU ONLY YOU ARE IN CONTROL OF YOU ONLY YO

ROL OF YOU ONLY YOU ARE IN CONTROL OF YOU ONLY
OF YOU ONLY YOU ARE IN CONTROL OF YOU ONLY YOU
OU ONLY YOU ARE IN CONTROL OF YOU ONLY YOU ARE
ONLY YOU ARE IN CONTROL OF YOU ONLY YOU ARE IN
OU ARE IN CONTROL OF YOU ONLY YOU ARE IN CONTROL
E IN CONTROL OF YOU ONLY YOU ARE IN CONTROL OF
CONTROL OF YOU ONLY YOU ARE IN CONTROL OF YOU
ROL OF YOU ONLY YOU ARE IN CONTROL OF YOU ONLY
OF YOU ONLY YOU ARE IN CONTROL OF YOU ONLY YOU
ARE IN CONTROL OF YOU ONLY YOU ARE IN CONTROL
E IN CONTROL OF YOU ONLY YOU ARE IN CONTROL OF
CONTROL OF YOU ONLY YOU ARE IN CONTROL OF YOU
ROL OF YOU ONLY YOU ARE IN CONTROL OF YOU ONLY
OF YOU ONLY YOU ARE IN CONTROL OF YOU ONLY YOU
OU ONLY YOU ARE IN CONTROL OF YOU ONLY YOU ARE
ONLY YOU ARE IN CONTROL OF YOU ONLY YOU ARE IN
OU ARE IN CONTROL OF YOU ONLY YOU ARE IN CONTROL
E IN CONTROL OF YOU ONLY YOU ARE IN CONTROL OF
CONTROL OF YOU ONLY YOU ARE IN CONTROL OF YOU
ROL OF YOU ONLY YOU ARE IN CONTROL OF YOU ONLY
OF YOU ONLY YOU ARE IN CONTROL OF YOU ONLY YOU
OU ONLY YOU ARE IN CONTROL OF YOU ONLY YOU ARE
NLY YOU ARE IN CONTROL OF YOU HAVE NO FEAR ONLY
OF YOU ONLY YOU ARE IN CONTROL OF YOU ONLY YOU
U ONLY YOU ARE IN CONTROL OF YOU ONLY YOU ARE IN
OU ARE IN CONTROL OF YOU ONLY YOU ARE IN CONTROL
E IN CONTROL OF YOU ONLY YOU ARE IN CONTROL OF

YOU ONLY YOU ARE IN CONTROL OF YOU ONLY YOU AI
ONLY YOU ARE IN CONTROL OF YOU ONLY YOU ARE IN
YOU ARE IN CONTROL OF YOU ONLY YOU ARE IN CONT
OF YOU ONLY YOU ARE IN CONTROL OF YOU ONLY YOU
ONLY YOU ARE IN CONTROL OF YOU ONLY YOU ARE IN
YOU ARE IN CONTROL OF YOU ONLY YOU ARE IN CONT
ARE IN CONTROL OF YOU ONLY YOU ARE IN CONTROL O
CONTROL OF YOU ONLY YOU ARE IN CONTROL OF YOU O
OF YOU ONLY YOU ARE IN CONTROL OF YOU ONLY YOU
ONLY YOU ARE IN CONTROL OF YOU ONLY YOU ARE IN
YOU ARE IN CONTROL OF YOU ONLY YOU ARE IN CONT
ARE IN CONTROL OF YOU ONLY YOU ARE IN CONTROL O
CONTROL OF YOU ONLY YOU ARE IN CONTROL OF YOU O
OF YOU ONLY YOU ARE IN CONTROL OF YOU ONLY YOU
ONLY YOU ARE IN CONTROL OF YOU ONLY YOU ARE IN
YOU ARE IN CONTROL OF YOU ONLY YOU ARE IN CONT
ARE IN CONTROL OF YOU ONLY YOU ARE IN CONTROL O
CONTROL OF YOU ONLY YOU ARE IN CONTROL OF YOU O
OF YOU ONLY YOU ARE IN CONTROL OF YOU ONLY YOU
ONLY YOU ARE IN CONTROL OF YOU ONLY YOU ARE IN
YOU ARE IN CONTROL OF YOU ONLY YOU ARE IN CONT
ONE LIFE, ONE LEGACY ARE IN CONTROL OF YOU ONLY Y
YOU ONLY YOU ARE IN CONTROL OF YOU ONLY YOU AI
ONLY YOU ARE IN CONTROL OF YOU ONLY YOU ARE IN
YOU ARE IN CONTROL OF YOU ONLY YOU ARE IN CONT
ARE IN CONTROL OF YOU ONLY YOU ARE IN CONTROL O
CONTROL OF YOU ONLY YOU ARE IN CONTROL OF YOU O

CONTROL OF YOU ONLY YOU ARE IN CONTROL OF YOU
ROL OF YOU ONLY YOU ARE IN CONTROL OF YOU ONLY
OF YOU ONLY YOU THIS TOO WILL PASS ARE IN CONTROL
N CONTROL OF YOU ONLY YOU ARE IN CONTROL OF YOU
ROL OF YOU ONLY YOU ARE IN CONTROL OF YOU ONLY
OF YOU ONLY YOU ARE IN CONTROL OF YOU ONLY YOU
U ONLY YOU ARE IN CONTROL OF YOU ONLY YOU ARE IN
OU ARE IN CONTROL OF YOU ONLY YOU ARE IN CONTROL
N CONTROL OF YOU ONLY YOU ARE IN CONTROL OF YOU
ROL OF YOU ONLY YOU ARE IN CONTROL OF YOU ONLY
OF YOU ONLY YOU ARE IN CONTROL OF YOU ONLY YOU
U ONLY YOU ARE IN CONTROL OF YOU ONLY YOU ARE IN
OU ARE IN CONTROL OF YOU ONLY YOU ARE IN CONTROL
N CONTROL OF YOU ONLY YOU ARE IN CONTROL OF YOU
TROL OF YOU ONLY YOU ARE IN CONTROL OF YOU ONLY
OF YOU ONLY YOU ARE IN CONTROL OF YOU ONLY YOU
U ONLY YOU ARE IN CONTROL OF YOU ONLY YOU ARE IN
OU ARE IN CONTROL OF YOU ONLY YOU ARE IN CONTROL
N CONTROL OF YOU ONLY YOU ARE IN CONTROL OF YOU
TROL OF YOU ONLY YOU ARE IN CONTROL OF YOU ONLY
OF YOU ONLY YOU ARE IN CONTROL OF YOU ONLY YOU
ARE IN CONTROL OF YOU ONLY YOU ARE IN CONTROL OF
CONTROL OF YOU ONLY YOU ARE IN CONTROL OF YOU
TROL OF YOU ONLY YOU ARE IN CONTROL OF YOU ONLY
OF YOU ONLY YOU ARE IN CONTROL OF YOU ONLY YOU
U ONLY YOU ARE IN CONTROL OF YOU ONLY YOU ARE IN
YOU ARE IN CONTROL OF YOU ONLY YOU ARE IN CONTROL

"A man is known by the
company he keeps."

—*Aesop's Fables*

"Dress up like Halloween and ghouls
will try to get in your pants."

—John Travolta in *Face/Off.*

Meganode 5 — The Company

THE HOUSE WAS ROCKING. About 40 kids, ages ranging from 15 to 18, were packed into my home. The kitchen was the hot spot where my dad's drum set and his beloved Stratocaster were cranked up and his Marshall amps were shaking the walls. But we had no worries. My parents were off on a four-day weekend.

When I was 16 and in high school, I'd already decided I was not going to take drugs or get drunk. I wasn't interested in that crowd, but when my folks decided to take the six-hour drive to Nova Scotia for a vacation, the pressure began to build. It was the first time I'd ever been trusted to be alone in the house. For all I knew it would be the last, so it did seem like a real opportunity. I was promised that no one would ever know, but I can't tell you what I was thinking that convinced me to go along with hosting a full-blown party. Peer pressure wears you down. You don't think of it as bullying, but when people make you do something you don't want to do, something you know better than to do, what do you call that? Bullying is a little bit like rape. Sometimes it's violent, even deadly. Sometimes it's just about getting needled until you can't say no anymore.

So I had a party on my hands and the party took the

usual course. By the time it was in full swing, only about a half dozen of the people there were really friends of mine. There was lots of drinking and smoking pot—the living room looked like a mini Woodstock. We hadn't posted anyone to keep watch, no reason to bother, but everyone had gotten hungry and someone called out for pizza. About 11 o'clock, the kid watching for the delivery man hollered in the door to me, "The pizza guy is here. Hey. He drives a white Toyota Camry, just like your folks."

I saw my whole life flash before my eyes—all 16 years of it—and I knew that everything I'd ever done was about to be called into question. I had about three minutes from that warning to when my parents actually came in the house. It was pitiful to watch as I attempted a one-man extreme home makeover, ditching the evidence as fast as I could tear through the house. I failed miserably.

Let me tell you some things about my dad. He worked hard for the things he owned and put great value on things he was able to buy, like his musical equipment. He wasn't a cool dad who would say, "kids will be kids" or take the time to remember that he'd fucked up plenty back when he was growing up. I had every right to be afraid.

Anyway, he threw everyone out, friends and strangers, until there was only me and I was in deep shit.

And that's the way it is with the company you keep. No matter what people say when they are hooking you up with their plans for your life, in the end, the consequences of your decisions always come back where they belong. Even when you are in a group, you have to make decisions for yourself, because the person who has to live with your decisions is you.

Who's on Board?

The company you keep is your Company. Your friends might be a motley crew. They might not be the kind of people you'd hire for your Fortune 500 business, but in the business of your life and your Legacy, they are already operating as your co-workers, your staff, your advisers and your suppliers, so you need to take a look around at who's on board and who is not and plan your strategy accordingly.

If the company you keep just wants to trash your house, and you let them, you have no one to blame but yourself. If you want more out of your life than parties and raising hell then you need to shut down that business ASAP, fire the whole bunch and start a new one. You need to hit that reset button.

That doesn't mean you only associate with church ladies and choir boys. And it doesn't mean you judge people based on their appearance (shit, look at me—I'd probably have a hard time getting a job at the bank that takes care of my money). And it doesn't mean that everyone has to fit in some kind of mold. You don't even have to like the people you hang around. You just need to know who they are, what their skills are, what their flaws are and act accordingly.

The CEO of every company has to work with people he or she would rather avoid: competitors, regulators, disgruntled former employees, deadbeats, family members without a clue, crazy people who wander in off the street and on and on. Not all of it is in your control.

This chapter is about the part you do control, about the people around you who share your mission, the ones you work with toward your personal and professional goals. It's also about the people who interfere and how to deal with them. There are lots of people in between those two extremes, casual friends, enemies or "frenemies"—which is to say "good influences," "bad influences" or "what the fuck." You owe it to yourself and to the Company you are building to have an idea where people fit into your big picture, because sometimes your biggest ally or your worst opponent can appear out of the blue. Sometimes the person you most need in a tight spot is just sitting there on the fringes of your relationships.

People are Important

The people in your life are simply your most important asset and potentially your biggest obstacle, so you need to be conscious of the potential. You'll still have as much time as you like for fun and games with friends and neighbors. And yeah, people aren't pieces you can move around on the game board of life, but you need to assemble your team carefully, make decisions on who is really in and who needs to stay on the margins.

Nobody goes it alone in the world, at least not if they are trying to do something that will last. Your Legacy is all yours, but you're going to need help to get there. You're going to need a partner or two. So to start off, you need to know who your partners are. Some of them are obvious, true life colleagues whom you have chosen and have chosen you back.

I sometimes tell people to take out their cell phones and go through the log of recent calls and texts. Flag anyone you've reached out to five times in a two-week period. You don't contact everyone by phone, so think about others who you turn to for counsel or for the material you need to make things happen in your life. Then list all of the people you know you could turn to if the shit hit the fan, the ones you'd actually seek out if a zombie plague swept the country. Don't forget to include the people who are first on your list to invite to go to that new blockbuster movie you're dying to see. People you enjoy knowing are usually the people with similar goals. They are comrades.

Choose your comrades wisely. Comrades can turn out to be partners.

But everybody matters, because people influence one another. You may not know it, but every day people change the way you think and act just by being around you.

You may think you make your own choices, good and bad, but as often as not, it's outside influences that get us into trouble. In scientific studies it's been shown that people usually were pressured into their worst behaviors. Here are just a few stats on how many people, on average, get bullied or otherwise pushed into their addictions and crimes: Smoking—38 percent; Drugs—53 percent; Alcohol—49 percent; Crime—56 percent.

And women and girls getting pressured into sex (and pregnancy ending in single-parent lives or abortion), that's practically off the charts.

It's not brain surgery (although many people do need to get their heads examined).

If you want to get into shape, don't share a couch with a couch potato.

If you are trying to quit smoking weed, don't carpool with Cheech and Chong.

If you are trying to build you own confidence, don't discuss your plans with someone who makes negativity and putting down other people their default position.

If you are trying to lose weight, you shouldn't hang out with the manager of the local Krispy Kreme.

If you aren't drinking, then why are you making weekend plans for the disco party at the Saturday Night Fever club?

If these examples sound ridiculous, I suggest you do a little self-evaluation. I bet you'll find at least a few examples of choices you are making in who you hang around that are just as asinine and counter-productive.

On the other hand, look at the things you are doing right. Maybe you are going to the gym, taking night courses for a new job, or maybe you play golf at a club where successful people have memberships.

What are you doing to connect with those people? When you see that guy with the perfect physique, are you too intimidated to just go up and say, "I'm new to this whole gym thing, but I'm really trying to make it work. Got any advice?" Some people are just jerks, but most people are happy to help, and what that guy knows could be your ticket to a lifetime of healthy living. Ask a question and get an answer. That's how it starts. He may not know it, but you just added him to your Company.

When you think about it, your Company includes a lot of people, and not all of them are aware that they are working for you or even with you, but you need to be aware of every one of them and the role they play. If you like, you can send them a note, later, and tell them that you are counting them in. See how they react.

The Art of Schmoozing

If you're thinking clearly about it, you realize that everybody you deal with for more than a minute or two is really part of your Company. You are either partners, you are working for them, or they are working for you. When you talk to the waitress at a restaurant it's easy to think it doesn't matter. And it won't unless you make it. The way you treat the people who are serving you can have a big effect on your life. Treat your server like a human being and you'll make a positive impression. Maybe only the waitress will notice. Maybe the people around you or at your table will notice. Maybe the next time you eat there with a potential partner, that waitress will recognize you and return the favor and make you seem special. Maybe nothing will happen, but it can't hurt and it's a great habit to have.

Treat people like they are special, because they are. This goes for hotel clerks, cashiers at the grocery store, taxi drivers, everyone. You may wonder, "Why? Those people don't care about me. We don't have anything in common." But everybody cares about themselves so if you take a moment to care about the people you meet you will have something in common. And you'll make a positive difference everywhere you go. You don't have to believe in Karma to know that's smart.

Good schmoozers know how to be charming but they also make other people feel like the center of attention. That's smart whether you're talking to the guy on the loading dock or the CEO.

But while you can treat everyone like part of your Company, you need to really limit the ones who are in your inner circle. For this group you need to be constantly hiring and firing because there's a limit. Facebook limits the number of "friends" you can have to 5,000, but everyone knows that's a joke.

A British anthropologist named Robin Dunbar studied apes and determined the number of meaningful relationships the average primate could maintain. He also studied primitive villages and tribes. He compiled that data, then calculated the average brain size of a chimp compared to a human and determined that people could have a stable social relationship with about 120 people.

OK, that's probably all a bunch of bullshit, but let's just go with that number. It sounds about right. Say you have approximately 120 people that you can consider to be your inner circle. People you can keep up with and care about.

When you think about it, that's not all that many. And remember, a lot of those spots are already taken by close family and friends, so when you are thinking about putting together a team, you need to be choosy.

There's a larger group of people in your life, too, outside that inner circle. These are the people you admire, that you allow to inspire you. They are the connections you make along the way, the hands you shake, the business cards you pick up, the people you know about who do the kinds of things you do. Maybe they do it better and can help you out or maybe you can offer them a hand and make an alliance. Each of those people is like a distant star with it's own planets, it's own solar system. Each of those people has his or her own set of friends and contacts, plans and resources.

Just because someone isn't in your inner circle doesn't mean they can't be important to you and you to them. You need to have a plan for how to reach those stars, and how to set up diplomatic relations between your worlds. Start doing business across the galaxy. That's how you make your own star bigger and stronger and turn it into a super star. That's how you take your Company intergalactic.

Back in 2004, Sir Richard Branson, the founder of the Virgin Group (think Virgin Mobile, Virgin Airline and a shitload of other companies) announced a deal with Microsoft co-founder Paul Allen and legendary aeronautical engineer Burt Rutan to create Virgin Galactic, the country's first space tourism company. They have plans for public space flights with tickets at about $200,000 a pop on Spaceship One and it looks like all systems are gonna be go, probably by the time you are reading this book.

There's a guy who thinks outside the box. Branson once said, "Business opportunities are like buses. There's always another one coming." But you've got to go where the buses are. You've got to keep your eyes open or you'll just be left standing there with your bus fare in you hand. New partners are like that, too. They come and go, but you've got to remember that each one could be a whole new universe of possibilities, if you have a plan and a vision you can share with someone who is ready and able to shoot for the stars.

Who Wins?

get letters all the time from people who want to give up. They've been bullied by people who don't even know them. They've been bullied by their "friends." We can not allow people to live life like this. We need to come together and make a stand, ensure people that change is possible, hope is real and passion lives inside of each of us. It breaks my heart when I get messages like these; it also fuels my motor even more. I know so many of us live in fear! We live so deep inside our souls we are scared to come out, so we punish ourselves. Not anymore. We are working hard to help anyone who is willing to put the time and energy in to change. That's the hope we must provide for one another. Otherwise, the bullies win.

Take things the other way for a minute, not to the stars but to the ground and below. Sometimes people are pure negativity. Sometimes rather than take you to the stars, they want you to go to Hell. And don't think they can't make you.

Like I said, bullying and peer pressure are not just kid games (or crimes). There are bullies everywhere in every level of business. Their tactics just get more devious and more sophisticated in the office or in the business world.

The Company I had around me for many years was constantly telling me *no*. They didn't care what I put in my body or who I slept with, but they said no to my biggest ideas, my best plans. People would hear what I had in mind for my band and look at me like I had three heads. Even after I succeeded with Recycled Percussion, when I told them about Legacy X, those same looks appeared. I just looked back at them and saw them as they were, people without the bravery to go after what they want out of life, people wearing horse blinders to the possibilities all around them. Now when I find people like that in my Company, I just fire them and find someone who shares my vision, because if someone you're traveling with can't see where you are going, they are just going to get in the way and trip you up.

A Dark Secret

I'm not saying I had everything right when I was first setting my path, but I knew where I wanted to go. It's hard to hear negativity from the people you love and care about the most. There's nothing worse than hearing your dad tell you that you are wrong. I eventually had to break away from the "No" bodies and make my own *yes*. Now I'm headlining on the Las Vegas Strip in a band that has generated millions of dollars in revenue. So let me share an important secret with you.

There is something in other people, even people who love you, that wants to cut you down when you are trying to rise. Even the best employees in your Company will want you to fail. Maybe it's just that inner competitiveness of people, but when you do poorly, other people feel better. When you do well, other people want to take you down a peg. Maybe it's just that people who love you don't want to see you pull away, change. Maybe it's just the test you have to go through to become a leader, to really take control, to be your own boss. It's not supposed to be easy, so the people around you, both friends and competitors, make it as hard as possible.

Try telling a friend you've been going out and getting shit-faced with the good news. You say, "Tommy, I'm quitting drinking, I'm focusing on some new things in my life." If Tommy is a friend, his reaction is usually, "Wow, good for you." But on the inside a switch goes off and the thought pops up, "He thinks he's better than me." What makes this so fucked up is that while you are trying to do something for yourself, Tommy makes it into something that's all about him. He may try to undermine you, maybe without even realizing what he's doing. He'll make fun of your choice and try to get you to laugh at yourself, get over it. I can't tell you why people act this way, but they do. I've seen it a hundred times and probably you have too.

Two things might happen. Tommy might actually see you are serious and start to take an inventory of his own drinking and his own choices. The more likely scenario is that Tommy will just find someone else to hit the bars with as soon as he can. You lose a friend, but you really win.

If this sounds a bit like war, well it is. It's a battle for your Legacy; your Company are your troops. You've got to stay in attack mode. Playing defense is OK for awhile, but in the long run it's a losing strategy. You've got to be aggressive about your choices, your relationships. You've got to pick your battles wisely and fight to win.

Never forget, it's *your* Legacy you are going for, so don't let others hold you back. Even people with the best of intentions can stand in the way. Letting the feelings of other people determine your most important decisions about your own life goal is suicide. You take the consequences and you obtain the benefits of the risks you take. And if you fail, you own it and move on. Failure isn't the end, it's a step along the way. Anyone afraid of failing is doomed to the worst kind of failure—never really having tried, never knowing what could be with a little vision and courage, never realizing your purpose and your potential, never creating your Legacy.

The friends and resources you work with every day, the concepts and strategies you have developed, your branding and goals, these are all elements of your Company. They serve as a reminder that no one does anything completely on their own. To succeed requires alliances, partners and preparation. Building your relationships and connecting with others who can help you on your path is a process full of dangers and rewards. But in the end, only you are in charge of you. As the owner of your Company, everything you do and every impression you make on others is part of your business model.

But nothing is more important to your future than the group of people you count as your team—your Company.

Actions

1. *Recognize That Your Company is Already Operating.*
   Start treating everyone you meet like part of your Company. Keep in close touch with your partners. Treat your employees with respect and interest. Treat those you work for like clients that you have to impress.
2. *Take an inventory of the people already in your life.*
   Imagine that, for the world, the shit hits the fan and you find yourself smack in the middle of the zombie apocalypse or a

nuclear holocaust. Who among all your friends do you want to have around to help you survive and rebuild?

Imagine you win the Megabucks. You've got a million a year for the rest of your life. Who do you know that you would trust to help you figure out what to do with that kind of money?

Imagine that you lose everything. Who would still be there for you and who would you partner with to start building your Legacy from scratch?

Those names are your inner circle. Hire them.

3. *Create an Organizational Chart.*

Take a big sheet of paper and put a circle in the middle with your name in it. Then, draw lines out to other circles all around it with the names of your closest friends and associates. Begin to picture how they fit into your Company, or if they even do. What role does each person play? There's nothing wrong with having a friend who is there just to have a good time or blow off some steam, but is that the only role that person plays? Make notes under their circles about what they bring to your Company. You'll begin to see areas you need to strengthen in your Company profile. Who advises you? Who motivates you? Who inspires you? Who holds you back? You can continue this process by making circles around your friends to include some of their closest friends and associates. Who in those circles would be a benefit to your Company? They are only one degree away from you. You may want to start cultivating some new partners.

Strategies

(Got a plan? A crazy idea? A way to fix the world?
Write that shit down and do it!)

"Who are you? I really want to know."

—The Who

"Early to bed, early to rise, work like hell and advertise."

—Ted Turner

Meganode 6 — The Brand

I'M WAITING FOR MY MOM to pick me up at my dad's house to take me home. I'm 14 years old. She's late, but I expected that. It's her standard operating procedure. She'd sometimes send someone else to get me, but I didn't expect to see the dilapidated 1970 pickup truck that pulled up to the house. Or the scrawny guy who leaned out and told me to climb in. I remember he had a scar from a bullet hole on the side of his head and when I looked in the cab I saw he had a big knife strapped to his belt and the dashboard was covered with a stretched deer hide. Oh, and I also remember his name. "Your mom sent me to pick you up," he said as he gestured for me to get in the truck. "I'm Skunk."

Don't get me wrong. I love my mom dearly. She's an amazing woman. Always made me feel special. Always made sure we had a great Christmas. I sometimes wonder if I'm the only one who sees that. For most people, she has allowed other things to define her: drinking, chronic lying, fucking up.

She's always been a free spirit, hasn't had a full-time job since she was in her mid-30s. She's incredibly giving, the kind of person who invites a homeless person to come sleep on the couch. On the other hand, she's always borrowing money from family members. She's cried wolf so long about her financial problems that no one cares anymore. No one believes her.

She's got such a soft heart she would adopt stray dogs, as many as 10 of them at one time, trying to save them all. But when our house burned down when I was 15, it was pretty obvious who did it and why. All the strays she had been taking care of had conveniently been moved out the day before.

Did I mention she was late? She made being late into an art form. She was late for my graduation. The trailer we lived in looked like what you might imagine if you were designing the set for a Hollywood movie about a drunken drug dealer. Cans and bottles everywhere, sometimes cocaine lines left out on the counter. Mom was the kind of drinker who was a sweetheart between beers one and six and a nightmare between beers seven and twelve.

Actually I sometimes wanted my mom to be late. When I knew she'd be picking me up from sports, I'd give her a time to come get me that would be after the guys had left. That way they wouldn't see her pull up drunk in our shitty old car. I guess you could say mother's Brand was worthless. If she was a penny stock, you wouldn't be able to convince the most naive NY stock exchange investor to buy into it.

There was someone else in my life who would come and pick me up. Sometimes on Fridays my uncle would pull up at the trailer park and take me to see wrestling or a rock concert. Sometimes we'd go to the beach or to the arcades. He always called me Sport. My uncle is just 10 years older than I am. He never drank, has never done drugs. He was student body president of UNH, got elected as a New Hampshire state legislator in his early 20s. He's a great dad, a coach. He treated people the way he wanted to be treated. Took time to understand people's needs. Never let people around him, friends or foes, force bad decisions on him. He represented leadership and strength. He had a conviction about doing what he believed in. He took calculated risks to improve his life as years went by.

I think a lot about those weekend trips with him. In retrospect, I know he saw what was happening to me and wanted to get me out of some situations—the kind that would tend to happen at my house over the weekends.

My uncle showed me an alternate path, a different way of life. As I said, I really love my mom and she helped make me who I am in lots of ways. But looking at the two descriptions above, I can also see which of those two models I decided to follow, which Brand earned my respect.

People are always selling themselves, always offering themselves to the world and seeing what they are worth. I learned the importance of this while promoting Recycled Percussion. There are a lot of guys out there who drum on buckets. We were professional, we treated people well, we delivered. When people started paying us a lot of money to perform, they knew we were worth it. We had a trust-worthy Brand.

You might think it's harsh to try to put a value like that on a person, but the truth is you do it all the time. Every time you decide who to hire or who to ask out on a date or who to hang around with you are shopping for something. If you were shopping for a role model, for the kind of person you wanted to be, and saw those two brands, my uncle and my mom, displayed on the shelf, which one would you buy?

OK, that's an easy question. Here's a harder one. If *you* were a brand displayed on a shelf, would you buy yourself?

Who the Fuck Are You?

The world is full of people. You see them everywhere you go—stadiums full of them. You scream at rock concerts along with thousands of them, you walk the streets in crowds of them, you squeeze into the middle seat in the airplane between two strangers. Maybe you wonder about them, about their lives. What makes them who they are? With so many people how is it possible for your life to stand out, or to even matter?

Sometimes we spend so much time wondering about other people, we forget to wonder about ourselves. Of all the people in the world, the one person you do not want to take for granted is yourself. The most famous philosopher of all time was a guy named Socrates. He said, "The unexamined life is not worth living." In other words if you aren't questioning your own life, examining it, trying to figure out how it works and where it's going, then it's basically just a piece of shit.

That's badass. That's the truth.

If you don't know who you are then no one does. If you don't take the time to figure out your own motives, your own strengths and weaknesses, your passions and your personal brand, then you are just heading for the remainder bin—the trash heap—the dump.

But let me be clear. A personal brand is not about ego or self-glorification. It's not about buying some clothes you think that other people will think look cool or edgy or hip hop or hippie or whatever kind of shit happens to be popular right now. It's about knowing who you are and what you represent. And while you can piss your life away without ever really knowing you have a brand, you still have one. Your brand is " Hey! I'm Pissing My Life Away." But really, a brand is not something you create. It's more like your DNA that reveals itself as you grow up. It's like a seed that's already planted. You just feed it, water it, give it some light and watch it blossom. Or not, and it dies and rots.

So ignore all the crap about "creating your brand" that's out there. There are whole books devoted to it, but here's the deal. Your brand should be as simple as breathing. Most of the time and effort you put into dressing up and styling yourself is probably doing more to hide it than reveal it. When you see someone you recognize a block away on the street, why do you recognize that person from all the millions of people it might be? Even if you can't see their face, you know the way they stand, the way they dress, the way they move. It's as unique and original as a signature. When you know a person, you know their brand, you recognize them.

The Brand is natural. It's just you. If you try to "create" it to be more like something the world wants from you, it's bullshit. Believe me, the people you are trying to impress most likely have excellent bullshit detectors. The kind of people you *want* to impress are people who know a good brand when they see it.

It's Not About Fitting In

It's not about fitting in. Your Brand isn't what makes you get along with others. That's why the military and the prisons, and some schools, spend a lot of time trying to get everyone to be as alike as possible, to get rid of the differences. It never really works, but they try, because to get a lot of people to follow a set of rules or to move them from one place to another it helps if they are uniform. That's why they grow square hard tomatoes, so they can pack more of them into a box. That's why they have to work at it so hard, to keep people in line, in order and in the same image.

Keeping things in line can be powerful. That's how the

Army fights wars and how a marching band can fill a whole stadium with music.

There's a different kind of power that comes from people who are individuals. There's a special beauty to people looking the way they want to look, doing the things they were made to do. There's also an important lesson about what you are worth as an individual.

Get this: You are priceless. There's no amount of money in the world that's worth your life. And yet that's true for every one of the billions of people on Earth. Each and every one of us is worth more than all the gold in Fort Knox. But we treat each other (and sometimes ourselves) like we're all worthless.

Having a Brand that you are proud of, that stands for something, is giving the finger to anyone who thinks you are worthless.

Think of a bag of marbles, you know those glass balls that kids used to play with in the dirt. Maybe they still do play with marbles. I hope they do. Anyway, the beauty of marbles is that there are different kinds, clear ones, solid color ones, ones with glass swirls in them, some bigger, some smaller, some chipped or weird in some way, but each one is different. Each one is cool to look at, but put them all together and the whole bag is totally beautiful.

People are like a bag of marbles, all different, but no one is better or worse than anyone else, and its all those little differences that make the whole thing beautiful. You make the world a cooler and more interesting place by being just who you are and being proud of who you are.

It's just revealing your true self to the world, and it's not just about being colorful. It's about meaning and value. Your meaning and your value.

Find a Dollar Bill

Imagine a blank envelope on the ground. It's probably just a piece of trash, easy to ignore. Put a name and address on it and people start to notice; maybe it belongs to someone, but most likely they'll still just walk on by. But leave a dollar bill sticking out and what happens? It's not a lot of money, but you can bet people will pick it up, check it out, remember it, tell people about it. "Hey, guess what I found! A dollar bill." They'll probably brag about it when they get home.

A little true value goes a long way. How much more valuable is the true you than a dollar bill? Your Brand is your value, your character, what you bring to the table. You need to know what it is and let other people know. You need to let them see your dollar bill sticking out, or your twenty or whatever value you've got.

You get an idea of what you're worth when you take a personal inventory, but then the message gets lost in the background noise of every day. And it's easy to lose sight of your worth, to get sidetracked trying to be things

You Need To . . .

You are more than what you do, but what you do defines you for others. It is important that when met with tragedy, obstacles, adversity, and the unexpected blows life hurls our way, we look deep into ourselves to not only find reasons to live but to still live those reasons. I've personally always believed that circumstances, regardless of how devastating they seem at the moment, will pass. Opportunities will blossom and once again you will be back in the fight. We just need to make sure that we don't forget to breathe, to live and *most* importantly to do our best treating ones we care about properly in that process. Life gets stressful for all of us. Try living through that stress by smiling on your inside at the thought of the current chaos passing. I can tell you this for a *fact*. Anyone involved with Legacy X will experience an overwhelming sense of community and purpose. You will be exposed to helping others in a way that hasn't been done before. What we are creating isn't a temporary solution or a band-aid to an issue. We are creating a movement that will last beyond our years. Get involved, be a part of the early stages of what will be an incredible journey!

you aren't just to please other people who are trying to be things that they aren't.

It goes back to the original question: Who are you now, and who are you really?

Here's the main thing. All that Mr. Rogers stuff about how you are special? It's true. You really are special. You are absolutely unique, just as identifiable as your fingerprint. You have within you the capability to present a global brand unlike any other on the entire planet. Like I said before, the question is who would buy it? Would *you* buy it? If you saw your Brand at the mall like a coat or a hat, would you even stop and try it on?

Being unique isn't the problem. Being unique is the most common thing in the world. You are unique like everyone else. What's important is being complete. You're only part way there. You've got a goal. You need to get a target lock on your Legacy and stay on course until you attain it. Along the way, your stock increases. Your worth on the market rises. Sometimes it takes years to get to where you can market what you have to share with the world. Sometimes it comes in one big burst, an overnight sensation. Sometimes you burn out, but not if you keep your eye on your Legacy. Because it's not about selling yourself. Even though you have a world-class brand, one that's desired, imitated, maybe even ripped off, it's never about what other people think of you. Its about how true you are to yourself.

It's a kind of a paradox. The less you worry about what other people think and focus on who you really are, the more people will tend to think of you, think about you. The less you need the approval of other people, the easier it is to get.

So, once again, it's time to hit the reset button. Do an inventory. Start with a clean slate. Don't worry, you won't lose anything, because the real you is what's underneath all the crap that gets piled on you by other people. It's under all those masks you wear to make other people like you, even though the people you fool aren't really worth knowing and the ones you want to know aren't fooled.

Projection Sucks

Here's something important you need to know.

People who don't know their own Brand will often try to turn you into someone you aren't. They might try to make you a hero or a bad guy. They might think you're a star who can't do anything wrong and the next minute they blame you for shit that's really coming straight out of their own minds. It's something that psychologists called "projection." They project themselves on other people and try to remake them in their own image. That's just the way people are. Maybe it makes them feel less lonely. Maybe it's how they test out their own personality quirks. Whatever it is, it's usually not healthy. Sometimes it's dangerous. When people project on you and you don't live up to their

131

expectations, they try to take you down. They blame you for their own problems.

Projection is why famous people hire bodyguards, but you don't have to be John Lennon for someone to decide that you are some kind of a saint or a demon. People who don't have any idea who they are tend to build their lives around other people and that's where the trouble begins.

If you think you'll get power or style or popularity out of acting like someone else, or making someone else into something they aren't then you are bullshitting no one but yourself.

People who want to use you will try to fit you into a box like a square tomato.

It's not just people trying to fit you into a mold, it's pretty much the entire commercial world. Marketing companies spend millions trying to get inside your head to sell you a vision of the world that includes their products. They do this by reprogramming your brain. They get you to associate something good, like sex or fun or power, with exactly what they have to sell.

Groups do the same thing. They want you to join them to get your fun, or your power, or your sex appeal. They try to replace your identity with their own vision of what's cool or trendy or good. This is true of small groups, like clubs and fraternities, and big groups like governments and religions. Some have great ideas, some are worth joining, but none is worth giving up your self. If you let some group take control of your self image, you are basically just flushing the most important thing you possess down the toilet.

The truth is that you are born unique, but forces in the world wear that down to fit you into a mold. Your Brand is you saying no. It's *you* deciding what makes you remarkable. It's the goal, the vision, the standards you set for yourself and the talents and tools you have at your disposal. It's identifying yourself as an entity of strength and power. So who are you? First know who you are by committing yourself to your Legacy. Then the way you present who you are to others will reveal your value and attract people and opportunities.

It's a guarantee, because who you really are is even more than you think. You just need to let the real *you* out and things will start to get interesting fast.

Actions

1. *Create a personal mission statement.*

   Take some time to write it out right now. What are you here to do? Where are you trying to get to? How will you know when you get there? Keep it short. Refine it. Memorize it. Live by it. When you lose your way, come back to it. Make it into the definition of your Brand. Live it so fully that if someone was to describe you to someone else, they would basically just recite your mission statement.

2. *For one day, keep your word.*

   Do you do everything you say you're going to do? How valuable is your word? If you tell someone you'll do something, do they believe you? Opinions are just words. If you want someone to value your opinion, first convince them to trust that your words are backed up by actions, that you do what you say you'll do.

3. *Make a great first impression on someone.*

   What's the first impression you want to make on other people? You've probably heard all your life that the first impression you make is the one people remember. Did it ever occur to you that this is true? If the impression that you give to other people is that you don't give a shit, then just make sure that's really what you want them to think, because that's exactly what they *will* think about you until you convince them otherwise. Find someone you want to impress and impress them.

Strategies

(Got a plan? A crazy idea? A way to fix the world?
Write that shit down and do it!)

"Where there's a will, there's a way."

—Old English Proverb

"Well I won't back down,
no I won't back down.
You could stand me up at the gates of hell
But I won't back down."

—Tom Petty

Meganode 7 — The Will

IT WAS 3 A.M. AND I WAS WEARING my pajamas when mom slipped me out the window of my room onto the snowy lawn. She told me to hurry. I ran through the dark to the neighbors' house where my instructions were to wake them up and have them call the police. If they asked me why, I was supposed to let them know that our phone had been ripped out of the wall.

A lot of thoughts and emotions ran through my adolescent brain as I made tracks in the snow that night. Mostly I was embarrassed.

When I tell people I've never had a drink, not even a beer, they often ask, "Why is that?" I don't usually give them the complete answer. It's a long story.

I remember lots of times riding in the back seat of my mom's maroon Chevy Nova on the familiar back roads of New Hampshire. I was so small I had to sit up to look out the windows, but I recognized the bumps in the road well enough that I usually knew just how much longer I had until we got home and all hell would break loose.

We'd be on our way back from one of our regular outings. My parents would have been partying at some clearing out in the back woods, drinking and smoking pot, while I'd run through the forest playing hide and seek with my friends. I never really knew what set them off, but I could always tell. It wasn't what they said, it was the quiet patches that made it clear something was up. My mom and my step dad wouldn't talk and then they'd argue about whatever it is that drunk people argue about. It was clear they were holding something in. Sharpening their knives. You could feel the tension. When we pulled up in the driveway around midnight, I'd head inside and get ready for bed and the two of them would start to face off.

The yelling soon would turn into banging and crashing. Something would hit the wall and echo like a drumhead. I'd lie in bed, alone, wishing that the covers over my head would muffle the sound so I couldn't follow the details of the fight. I knew most of the dialog. I had it memorized. It was like reruns from hell.

Even when I couldn't hear the words, I knew the pattern. After the first shouting there would just be some words going back and forth. Then quarreling. Then one voice would get loud while the other got quiet, usually that was my mom. She would seem to be drawing my step dad out, pissing him off even more by refusing to argue back, but finally both of them would be going at it full bore. When the crashing finally stopped, the echoing silence in the house was somehow even louder than the fight, so it took a while for me to finally go to sleep. And then, sometimes, the cops would come.

This was the mid-1980s and it's hard to believe it now. Two drunk parents driving home, kid unbuckled in the back. Cops coming over regularly, sometimes called by the neighbors, crunching through broken glass to question my parents and then having to decide which of them to take to the station while the other one cooled down. Today, I'd be pulled out of that home so fucking fast my head would be spinning.

I never invited friends over. I had no idea what kind of scene they would find when they arrived.

That was my life.

When people ask me why I don't drink, I don't usually tell them all that. I just say I took an oath at 15 that I'd never drink an alcoholic beverage. I tell them that sometimes it takes something drastic to give you that kind of will.

Sometimes it's the bad stuff that helps you get strong, but I don't recommend it. You just have to work with what you're given and do the best you can with what you've got.

That's where the Will comes in.

No Excuses

Welcome to the No Excuses chapter of Legacy X. The Will is not about trying. It's about achieving and maintaining.

The Will is a muscle. You exercise it and it grows strong and hard. You ignore it and it turns into a bunch of flab.

It figures that the vital ingredient in achieving your own personal Legacy is something that comes from within you. I'm not talking about "willpower" or something you use to stop yourself from having a second piece of birthday cake. I'm, talking about the ultimate commitment to yourself and your goals through the highs and the lows of your entrepreneurship. You can't allow failure, or success, to derail you. Your dedication is to your ideal self and it's always a work in progress.

Most of what and who you are, both the good parts and the bad, was given to you. You got it in your DNA or from the way you were raised. Some of it came from the teachers you had, the friends you made who influenced you to either do dumb shit or to get smart or be cool. But that's all in the past. You know that a lot of what makes you who you are is the choices you made, the paths you went down, but you may not have really known where you were going at the time. Now you do. So no more excuses.

The excuses have to stop somewhere, sometime. The time and place is now. You have to start to make your own decisions about who you are and who you will be.

Good thing you've got a tool that smashes excuses.

If you are a sculptor working on a big piece of granite, you've got a hammer and a chisel. If you are a musician working on classic riff you've got a guitar. If you're a plumber working on a stuck drain you've got a plunger and a pipe wrench. If you're a person working on your Legacy, you've got your will. It's the chisel you use to shape your future.

OK, sometimes it's more like playing whack-a-mole than like chiseling a statue, but a good game of whacking moles can help you develop your wrist action, hand-eye coordination. You never waste time when you are using your Will.

The Will is something you already have, but you had it all along when you were making bad decisions or just drifting. Like I said, it's like a muscle you're born with, but if you rarely use it, it might be too weak at first to make much of an impression. You need to make it strong. Fully developed, it's not just the most powerful weapon in your arsenal, it's the ammunition for every weapon, the nails for every hammer, the dynamite for every demolition. When it's switched on, it can provide a laser-like focus and give you the courage to trust yourself. When it's switched off, or ignored, it's as useless as a banana peel.

The Will is the opposite of the excuse. An excuse is cover for failure. The Will is a tool for success.

And every success, even a small one, is a boost that can have a huge effect on your path. What's hard at the beginning will get easier as you go.

You probably have some good habits that you drilled into yourself along the way. Some of these you don't even think about. They are just part of who you are. Your Will helped you build those habits and now they are permanent parts of your Machine. But the same is true of every failure. Allowing yourself to fail sets up patterns that seem just as permanent. Fail at something long enough and you start to think of your failures as who you are. That's why the instructions at the beginning of the book were so clear. Don't start down this road unless you are ready to go all the way.

Remember that test at the beginning of this book (the paper). That was to ensure that you are really prepared to do anything necessary to transform your life. To go half way is to accept failure as part of your life. That's unacceptable. That's not how you build a Legacy.

You May Have to Start at the Bottom

In alcohol and drug abuse there's a place known as rock bottom. That's the point at which a person has nowhere to go but up. I say that only you can decide what's your rock bottom, your turning point. You make that decision with your Will.

You know what it's like to turn over a new leaf, quit smoking, get in shape, start practicing guitar, or learn a new language. You start with a positive attitude, convinced that you can make the commitment you need and that you'll commit the time it takes to do it. And it feels good for awhile. You really start to feel things changing.

Then you quit. You go back to square one. You buy another pack of smokes or eat half a cake while watching TV. It's almost like you know it's going to happen, like a pattern you can't break.

The problem is that you are trying to do the wrong thing. You are *trying* to do something when what you need is just to *do* it. The secret to doing anything that makes a change is not how hard you try, it's about your fundamental commitment. Fundamental means it's the foundation. Are you committed or are you just blowing smoke? Without a foundation, things come crashing down when you least expect it. With a foundation you can build something designed to last.

Set a Date

If you are underwater and it's going to take 60 seconds to get to the surface, you don't give up and try to breathe halfway to the air. You determine that you'll wait because your life depends on it. It's time to realize your goals are just as important as your life. In fact, your Legacy is more important than anything in your life because it's the reason you are alive. You've got to determine that you'll do what it takes to keep your commitment to your goals. Your plans to get in shape, to make yourself a better person, to use your talents to the maximum degree, these aren't options. They are absolutely necessary to keep your Legacy alive. You've got to quit selling yourself short. You've got to stop trying to breathe when you're still underwater.

You've got to know how far it is to the surface—to your goals—and maintain until you get there. Think about it.

Your goal isn't to quit smoking for a few days. That's not even enough time to get the stink out of your clothes, but if that's as far down the road as you are willing to commit, then that's all you're going to do. I say quit right now, never look back. You'll thank me later. But not everyone thinks the way I think. If you've never quit before, maybe it makes sense to quit for three days, then three more, then three more. If that's your plan, then use your Will and work it. Just don't bullshit yourself.

If you don't have a plan, a commitment in place, then you're just screwing around. If you don't decide up front how long you are going to maintain, then as soon as the going gets tough, you bail.

Set a real goal, an actual length of time that you know will be enough to make the change and then stick to it and the change will happen. The Will needs a plan to work.

If you are working with a plan, with real commitments, you can adjust. If you have a real time in mind from the beginning and then mess up, at least you will know how close you came (or how early you fucked up). Setting a date means you are serious. If you get engaged to the girl of your dreams, what's the first thing you do? You set a date for the wedding. It's what makes the engagement a real thing. Same thing is true for getting engaged with a new you, turning yourself into the kind of person you need to be.

Treadmill of Death

'm laying in my bed, fan blowing to the left of me, ears still lightly ringing from the children screaming today at the assembly after I played drums for them, and my thoughts are all on *you*. I can't stop thinking about *you*. As I think about you I wonder if I am really thinking about me in the deep. I'm thinking how to maintain! How to continue to push forward as we make changes. Even making small changes is like walking around in ski boots. We try so hard at our respective goals only to have those around us laugh at us—if not out loud we can still sense it—to have doors slammed in our faces with the word "*No*" branded on the front, to feel like we don't make progress. It's like we are walking up the escalator on the wrong side. It can feel like we are on life's giant treadmill of hopelessness. But I know as I lay here that that treadmill does have a finish line, that those people laughing will become envious while you smile at your achievements, that the escalator eventually does shut down, allowing you to walk to the top without a problem. It only seems hopeless because most people give up before they ever see those results; they just give in, before they reach that summit. They pick up that drink, go back to that abusive relationship, back out of that career, start smoking again, stop working out and flat out just give up. Sure, they assume they will try again another day when they have the energy. Well this opens the door to failure and here's a secret: failure is the electricity that powers the treadmill of death. So what do you do? I have to tell you there is no "answer." We just wake up tomorrow, jump on that saddle, despite how sore we are from yesterday's ride, and push forward without looking back. We repeat that over and over and over and over and over again. I don't know when your success becomes a reality but I do know if you do not waver, it does.

How Long is Long Enough?

Different goals take different amounts of time, but there are some rules of thumb.

Physical trainers and psychologists say it takes about three weeks of steady practice to make something into a habit.

A good habit is a good thing, but it's still not permanent. Once something is a habit it's easier, but you can still fall back into old patterns.

If you can keep a habit going for a year it becomes a pattern in your life. You have made it a part of what you do in every season. You've hit a few curve balls off of it and tested it against the kinds of crazy shit that happens in your life. It's pretty solid. It's more than a habit now, it's a part of your nature.

Scientists say that about every five years you completely replace every cell in your body. As far as your flesh and blood and bones and brains are concerned, you are a new person. If you can hold onto a good habit for five years, it's not just a part of your nature, it's a part of you. It happened because you made it happen. It's a part of yourself that you created on your own. Maintaining is building yourself into the kind of person you want to be, the kind of person who can do things that the old you couldn't dream of doing.

It's the Will that can sculpt you into a new person. The numbers are just measurements for how far you've come.

A guy named Malcolm Gladwell has written a bunch of books with titles like *Blink*, and *The Tipping Point*. The ideas in his books get talked about a lot by people who've never read them. One of his ideas is called "10,000 Hours of Practice." That's what he says is required to become a master of something worthwhile, like playing a concert violin or becoming a computer programmer. He might be right, but really, most of these numbers were just pulled out of someone's ass (even Malcolm Gladwell). But they can help you focus, so use them. And always remember, the true goal isn't to hold out for a week or a year or five years. The goal is to change for good. That's your Legacy.

By the way, a word of warning. Use numbers but don't let them fool you. Copywriters use numbers to make things sound solid and important. Authors put them on their book covers.

Drink a bottle of 5-Hour Energy and check it out with a stopwatch. Read a book on 8-Minute Abs and you'll realize that's bullshit. (Everyone knows good abs take nine minutes.) "Quit Smoking in 30 Days"? Really? How about just quit smoking right now? Go to the garbage can and throw away those things that are hurting you. Don't let numbers screw with you. Use them. Don't buy into trendy bullshit.

Bullshit is the opposite of Legacy.

The Legacy is what remains of your life when all the bullshit is gone. It's the stuff you dreamed and built and maintained until it was a part of you. But it's not enough just to dream or just to build, you've got to maintain. Do something once and you learn. Do it twice and you get good. Do it long enough and you can teach it to someone else. But if you maintain, hold on to something long enough, it becomes a part of you. It strengthens you. Maintaining takes something hard and makes it natural, second nature.

A New First Day

It always starts with the first day you walk into the gym or a class—something that has made you insecure to try since day one. But you kickstart that stored-up energy and make a commitment to yourself that you will hold yourself accountable towards your goals. Then in the snap of a finger the first 5 pounds falls off, then a week later it's 10–15 pounds. You're hooked! You are doing things you thought you would never and could never do. A month later it's 20 pounds and so on. Eventually this becomes habit, a place of solitude, building strength mentally with every day you don't look back. This isn't a 90-day program, it's your life, it's your body and you take care of it the best *you* can as it helps prepare you for the roller coaster we call life.

Just because you have given up, or failed at something before doesn't mean it's over. It's not over until it's over. Starting over is a big part of maintaining. In fact, it's the main part, because no matter how much success or failure you pack into a day, each day is a new start.

Starting something is like opening a can of soda. There's power just popping the top. It's exciting taking that first fizzy sip. But after the fizz dies and the excitement runs out, where are you? You have to know this will happen and prepare for it. Have a backup plan.

Like I mentioned in the chapter on the Machine, you sometimes have to set things up so you can't just back out of your plans. Using your Will sometimes means planning for the times when the will is weak.

First of all, remember you aren't doing this to impress anyone else. You are doing it for you.

Remember you need an edge to achieve your goals. Every little success, every advantage you give yourself counts.

Prepare yourself for the comments of those around you. Don't ask me why, but people seem determined to make you fail when you try to change. Maybe it makes them uncomfortable about their own lack of will, but whatever it is, be prepared. Have a mental routine that allows you to listen to doubt and criticism (both are really forms of bullying) and just smile as it goes in one ear and out the other.

If you think you'll need a cigarette or a beer after a hard day, choose something else you can do; have a haven you can escape to. I used a bowling alley. Find your own safe place where you can do something healthy that you enjoy.

Get Radical

Don't be afraid to get radical.

Rent a locker at the gym and leave things there that you'll need the next day. Get a stack of $10 bills from the bank and every time you miss a workout, flush one of them down the toilet. If you can't stop snacking, stop bringing snack food into the house. If you have a roommate who insists on keeping bags of candy and chips around, find a locker and have them store their junk food there under lock and key.

Will isn't just about the moment. You can use your Will to make things easier for you in the future, too.

I remember going to school with a girl, she was probably 12 years old, she had a terrible habit of biting her fingernails. They were always ragged, sometimes bleeding. One day she got on the bus and there was Scotch tape wrapped around each of her fingertips. I asked her what that was all about and she said her parents had told her to do it every day for a month, to help her break the habit.

It may have seemed weird to the other kids, but to me it was genius. If you can't just quit doing something that's bad for you, then why not figure out a way to trick yourself into changing your behavior? Make it easier not to do it. That's probably where I got the idea to lock up my wallet at the gym at night, or to live somewhere without a shower, so I had no choice but to use the one at the place where I worked out.

That's my life. How about yours? You know your own weaknesses better than anyone. You may not be able to overcome every temptation that you experience, but you know the tricks that they play with your mind. So you've got the power to turn the tables on temptations and weaknesses. Come up with your own plans for radical maintaining.

In the movie *Memento*, the lead character has no short-term memory and he's trying to solve the mystery of the murder of his wife. Every day he wakes up he remembers nothing of the day before, so he has to leave himself notes, clues, reminders everywhere he goes. He even tattoos instructions to himself on his own body.

Radical, yes, but if that's what it takes, do it. You have a murder mystery to solve as well. Someone is trying to murder your Legacy with bad habits and addictions. Someone is trying to waste the precious days of your life. The murderer is the old you, the part of you that's dead already, the living corpse, the zombie you are trying to leave behind, but that person won't go quietly. You've got to fight to escape. It's time to be creative.

Your new life—and your Legacy—depend on it.

Actions

Starting Over for the Last Time (Again)

1. Will yourself to hit the reset button and make a new commitment to your Legacy;

2. Take an inventory. Be honest with yourself why and how you failed in your previous attempts;

3. Have a plan to overcome whatever it is that caused you to fail.

4. Set your checkpoints, your goals, with realistic dates and times so you'll have a way to measure your progress.

5. Fix it in your mind that if you don't make it to your checkpoint, you'll die.

6. Remember that even if you don't make it and you die, you can probably start over one more time.

7. Remember that eventually you run out of time.

Strategies

(Got a plan? A crazy idea? A way to fix the world?
Write that shit down and do it!)

_____

_____

_____

_____

_____

_____

_____

_____

_____

_____

_____

_____

_____

_____

_____

_____

_____

_____

_____

_____

_____

_____

_____

"Genius is talent set of fire by courage."

—Henry Van Dyke

"Let me stand next to your fire."

—Jimi Hendrix

Meganode 8 — The Fire

I WAS THE OWNER OF A COMPANY that didn't exist. I mean, it existed in my mind, but whenever I told people about it they would look at me funny or just walk away. I couldn't understand why they couldn't see it as clearly as I did. I could explain it to them in detail. They could tell how exciting I thought it was, how important I knew it was. Some people were interested if they listened long enough, but in the end, they'd walk away too.

Legacy X has been real to me for many years. I've been working on the designs, on the principles, on the moving parts of this organization since I was just a kid. Hell, maybe since I was born.

I knew it could help people, change their lives, change the world, but whenever I tried to get some people involved it was like the vision that was so bright in my eyes became a mirage and just disappeared. Lots of things are like that. People call them dreams. I really hate that word. Dreams. People use it to mean a lot of things, but what it means to me is stuff that only happens on the inside of your head. In your dreams you can go to the bottom of the ocean or fly over the trees. Try that in real life and you'll know there's not much difference between a dream and a fantasy—or a lie. Try to make your dreams come true without doing some hard work and you'll just wind up all wet or with some broken bones.

What gets me is how many people "dream" about things that they can do right now. I know lots of people dream about what it would be like to be in shape. To fit into nice clothes. To feel better and have more energy. Some people dream about what it would be like to quit smoking or dump some other bad habit. They think about it and even make some plans. Maybe they buy some books or DVDs or sign up for a program.

The Problem with Dreaming

That's the problem with dreaming. It doesn't get anything done, but it sells a lot of books and self-help programs.

How's this for a program? Want to stop smoking? Throw your cigarettes into the garbage disposal and hit "grind." Want to get off the couch and get in shape? Put down this book and go for a walk. Walk until you're good and sweaty. Do that every day. Walk to the mall and buy yourself a good pair of running shoes. Run to the gym and sign up. Making plans is fine, but it's not acting. And why make plans to do something you can do immediately? Unless you're just putting it off?

I know how this works. I did it myself. One day I realized I'd been thinking and talking about Legacy X so long that maybe it was really just a dream. Did I tell you I don't like dreams? Imagine me realizing that the one thing that excited me more than anything else might be just that—a stupid dream that would disappear the minute I woke up.

So I broke out the newspaper, looked up the real estate section and bought an office for my company that didn't exist. Guess what. It became real. The minute I had to figure out how to pay the rent and the electric bills it became even more real. I knew I had to hold myself financially accountable. The spark I'd been carrying around for so long that it almost went out, suddenly got brighter.

Our brains are programmed to postpone, to overthink things. That's usually a good thing. It keeps us from being stupid, walking out on thin ice or running into the traffic, but sometimes it just keeps us in our safety zone. To really get things done you have to break out of that knee-jerk programming. You have to look first, sure, but then you have to make the leap. If you're leaping off a bridge, you want to think about it for awhile, first. You could be jumping into danger. But if you're already in danger, you may need to jump fast. Jump now.

If you've been dreaming about doing something important to you, you are in danger. Time will suck the life out of that thing and turn it into a ghost that can haunt you forever. If you want to save that thing that's in your heart you don't dream. You act. You leap.

The hardest and most critical part of anything you do for your Legacy is starting. In fact, it's the only part.

Everything you do is just a series of starting points. Every day when you wake up you have to start again. Learn how to start and you learn how to succeed.

No one promised me a Las Vegas headline show. No one promised me that "company that didn't exist." No one promises you your Legacy, but you can be inspired by the accomplishments of others. I want my Legacy to be a new beginning for you. I want it to start a fire in your life.

The Fire Doesn't Wait

Fire happens now.

When someone yells "Fire," you move. If you are at a shooting range you pull the trigger. If you are in a crowded building, you get out. One way or another you act. If you wait a second too long, you might never get out alive. If you have a target in your sights and you hesitate for an instant, you miss. The best photographers in the world are the ones who don't wait to think about the right moment to click the shutter—they have trained their hands to think for themselves. That's how they capture that split second when the magic happens. That's how an Olympic archer knows just when to release an arrow from a moving bow, launch it through a slight breeze and still hit a 2.4 inch wide dot on a target that's 70 meters away. That's what the Fire is all about, being in the moment and acting in the moment.

More importantly, it's what makes the difference

between you deciding to do something and actually doing it. Sometimes you've got the best of intentions. You know it's time to get started on your Legacy, stop fucking around. You know where you want to go. You've got a plan to make things happen. You've got the motivation. You're truly inspired, revved up, ready to go. And what happens? Nothing.

Why? Who knows? You get distracted. A friend drops by. You overthink it. You get hungry, or need a nap. You drop back for a while and put it off. There's always tomorrow, right?

Wrong.

There's only today. Tomorrow is just a concept. Sometimes it's a useful one. It's good to plan for the future, to save up for the future—even if it never happens—but sometimes, in fact way too often, "tomorrow" is a lie we tell ourselves to avoid making a commitment to *now*.

We can tell ourselves some beautiful lies when we're really trying to put out the Fire.

Why put it out? Beats me. I think people are scared. Fire can be scary out in the world. It seems to have a life of its own. It's hard to control once it starts. The Fire inside you can be scary too, but it's really completely under your control. You can start it whenever you like and you can stop it just as fast. In fact, it's much easier to put it out than it is to get it going.

If you want to lose some pounds, you may have a

perfect weight in mind. Maybe you need to lose 50 pounds. You probably think that you'll be doing good when you lose the first ten pounds and better when you get half way there. When you step on the scale and see that you lost all 50 pounds, that will be a great moment. That will really be the big day. That all sounds true, but it's all backwards. The greatest moment isn't the last one. It's the first one, when you start to do what you've got to do to eat right and to start exercising and take care of yourself. Then the next greatest moment is the one after that, when you turn down that cupcake and decide to walk to work or watch less TV, and then the next greatest moment is the one after that.

Fire knows that every moment is great when you burn it up, use it for all it's worth, turn it into heat and light and power. Here's a secret known only to people who work with the Fire and aren't afraid to get their fingers burned a little. In the outside world, fire burns stuff up and turns it to ash. Inside you, the Fire makes its own fuel. It can take the ashes of your life and turn them into flesh and blood and give you more energy than you had to begin with.

Fire is pure action. It's not necessarily good or bad, but it gets things done. In fact, you could say it's the only thing that gets things done and it's up to you to make it good. Every choice you make, every dream you dream is just that, a dream, until you say go and strike a match, get off your ass, bust a move, take a chance.

It just takes a little fire.

More Than Aware

You need to be aware, but more than just that. Action is the first step in our shift from raising "awareness" to creating "solutions." What is a solution? When our time and energy begin to save lives (starting with your own). Your effect on the world around you is an unquantifiable statistic but we know it's making a difference. That's why we spend our time, energy and brain power to help that process. Don't you dare doubt *your* abilities. That doubt will prevent attempts that become success, in *all* aspects of life! Why should you always strive for positivity? Because the opposing mind-set is a terrible way to live and it's also the opposite of awareness. Awareness is just the beginning, but it's always positive. To be aware is to be able to begin to act. For those of you that are standing up for yourself and making positive things happen in your life, I salute you!

Where's the Fire?

So where do you get this fire? Good news. You've already got it. It's called being alive. You've had it since you were born and you'll have it until you die. When you use it, your life gets bigger, brighter. When you don't, it gets small, dim. Just like real fire, you can build it and it spreads. You can even light up people around you. You probably know people who make you want to do things, who inspire you to get out of the house and make a difference? Those people are fire starters. You probably also know people who put a wet blanket on you, smother your enthusiasm. It's up to you to decide what kind of people you want to be around. You choose your Company. It's also up to you to decide what kind of person you want to be.

Are you a fire builder or a fire smotherer? Do you encourage people you know, motivate them to get busy? Do you get excited about what they are doing or do you try to slow them down to your speed?

Fire can cook and fire can clean. Sometimes you need to turn up the heat to get things done. Other times you've got to start over, scorch the Earth.

You may not be able to set the world on fire right away. Start with what you know.

If you want to build a campfire you start small. All it takes is a spark and a tiny piece of fluff to get things going. Oh, yeah. It may take a lot of tries. And some knowledge, but keep trying long enough and the knowledge will come. If you ever watch someone try to start a fire by rubbing two sticks together, you'll know that that's not going to happen anytime soon, but you get the idea. Some techniques work better than others but heat always comes from action. Get smart about what you're doing and you can heat things up faster. You can get a blaze going just about anywhere.

Fire needs fuel. The fire in the belly, the kind of fire that changes you and your world from the inside out needs you to stop saying no. Fire wants to burn. Just stop putting it out and it will eventually blaze.

Just Three Things

Most everything in the world is one of three things, fire, fuel and ashes.

Fuel is all around you. It's in everything you want and every place you want to go. Ashes are the past. You can mess around with them all you want but you'll just get your hands dirty. Fire is Now. Fire is the urgency of your life, what keeps you moving. It's lighting a fuse or kindling for a wood stove or torching a bonfire. You can stare at the logs all day, but nothing happens without a little fire. And a little fire can make a big fire.

People talk about burning a candle at both ends like it's a problem, but a candle is made to burn and in the end, would you rather burn the whole candle up or wind up tossing half of it in the trash?

I don't like New Year's resolutions. Why wait? But since that's when we make promises to ourselves about the things we want to change, every year we make commitments to ourselves. To get in shape, to quit smoking, to quit drinking, to find ways to battle our depression or anxiety. We're going to find a new job. We're going to relinquish this unhealthy friendship, change relationships and change who we are and then . . . nothing. We come up with empty hands. Every year without fail, we fail. That cannot happen anymore. We can no longer make commitments to ourselves and then let ourselves down. It becomes status quo. Your ability to inspire yourself and to influence others dwindles every time that happens.

That's how a Legacy is lost. Not by failing, but by waiting.

Now's your chance. I'm here to say it's a new start.

With Legacy X you have a new start, a new support system, a new community of people who care. I'm here to say, this time around, don't fail. Rise up against all odds. Make a commitment to yourself that you can follow through on. Do it for yourself. Take back your life. It doesn't have to be a complete life overhaul the first day. You don't have to head up a mountain that's impossible to climb. It needs to be you saying here's what I want to do that's really important to me.

And then achieve it. Do it. Take hold of yourself. Make a commitment that you can follow through on and you become a part of something bigger, stronger than you were. Wake up in the morning with a smile, a sense of purpose and direction. This is your chance. Not tomorrow.

Right now.

Action

How to Set the World on Fire

You don't build a fire by holding a match to a log. Start with something small, get it burning, add something a little bigger and just don't stop until you've got the whole log burning. That's the same way you change the world, start small and start now and just keep going.

Step One: Decide one major thing you really want to do for your Legacy.

Step Two: Pick one thing you can do about it right now, not tomorrow.

Step Three: Do it.

Repeat as needed.

Strategies

(Got a plan? A crazy idea? A way to fix the world?
Write that shit down and do it!)

Some Final Words

Okay, that's enough for book one (there will be more).

In fact this page is enough. Tear it out and tape it to your bathroom mirror in case you need a reminder that time is ticking away, but it's time to stop reading.

In fact, stop thinking. Forget about your brain. It'll take care of itself. Start doing.

The more you think about something, the longer it takes to get started. Every second you aren't doing something to make things better is a second that things are getting worse. In life you either grow or you rot. There's no middle ground.

Choose to grow by doing. Choose how you grow by what you do.

If you want to be happy, smile. If you want to be scared, run away. If you want to be richer, set a higher dollar value for what you do. No one is going to give you a raise unless you ask for it. If you want to get someplace, hit the road. If you want to make a difference, have an opinion. It doesn't really matter if it's right or wrong, it's yours. You can change your mind later, but only if you have one to change. You can't do shit with someone else's ideas. Even with mine.

Anything you find useful in this book can be yours, but only when you start to do it. Until then, if you are just reading or thinking about it you're just fucking around. You're just borrowing. When you find something that's true, steal it, tape it to your mirror, make it your own and it will be as much a part of you as a hand or a foot. But even your hands and your feet have to get used or else they rot.

Here's my final words to you, my friends (for now).

Don't rot, grow.

Live.

One life, one Legacy.

THE END

Acknowledgment

For those who have inspired me to bring life to this book—
I will thank you in person.

—Justin Spencer

Rip It Out, Tape It Up, Send It In!

If you made it all the way through this book without marking it up and ripping stuff out then you did it wrong. Remember, this isn't a book, it's a tool. Get it dirty, use it up, scratch out stuff you disagree with, put your mark on it. Right now I want you to flip back through and find your favorite page. Tear it out. Make some copies of it and tape them up where they can remind you of your mission. Then send me a picture.

Justin@LegacyX.com